The FANTASTIC LIFE®

*How to Get It,
Live It, and Pass It On®*

R. Craig Coppola

Published by
Habanero Publishing LLC
6040 E Montecito Ave Scottsdale AZ 85251

Printed in the United States of America

First Edition: 2014

ISBN 978-0-9898672-2-1

To my wife Tracy and our amazing family, Brad Lemon, Dan Sullivan, and the countless other mentors who have helped me get to where I am today. Without you, my *Fantastic Life* would not have been possible.

Table of Contents

Acknowledgments ix

Foreword xi

Introduction 1

Rule #1   Know Your Story 9

Rule #2   Be Crystal Clear On What You Want 17

Rule #3   Build Your Résumé Every Year 25

Rule #4   All of Life is Connected 33

Rule #5   Make Sacrifices 41

Rule #6   Stay Out of the Matrix 47

Rule #7   Be Value Driven 53

Rule #8   Play Where You Can Win 61

Rule #9   Set Goals 69

Rule #10   Stay Out of The Gap™ 81

Rule #11   The Growth Paradigm 89

Rule #12   Get a Win 99

Rule #13   The 2% Rule 105

Rule #14   There are Two Kinds of Pain 113

Rule #15   Take the Decision Out of the Moment 119

Rule #16   Don't Waste Time 125

Rule #17   Life is About Opportunity, Too 133

Rule #18   Do Nothing In Moderation 139

About the Author 145

Acknowledgments

So many fantastic people helped make this book and the lessons in it a reality. Thank you to Jake Johnson for writing this with me. Another huge thank you to Dan Sullivan, my mentor and coach, who taught and continues to teach me some of the most important lessons in this book. My wife and family, for supporting me in all my endeavors. Finally to my daughter Kellie, for her keen eye in spotting mistakes and editing.

Foreword

After two decades of friendship, both professionally and socially, I will be the first to say that Craig Coppola's life is truly Fantastic. When I met him, he was just starting out in the business, and what immediately struck me was his passion and drive to be the best at everything he took on. Whether it was being a great father to his small children, getting the biggest return on a real estate investment, or accomplishing some ridiculous athletic achievement, Craig never settled for mediocre. His talent and drive were what drove me to make my first investment with him, and since then I have seen him succeed in almost everything he's put his mind to.

What impresses me most about Craig, however, are not the multiple achievements decorating his résumé. It is his immense passion for everything in life, from the smallest wins to the incredible feats. The attention and care he gives to every endeavor he takes on is unmatched in anyone I have ever met. Craig's drive and his vision have set him on the course for a *Fantastic Life*, one that I have watched grow enormously over the past twenty years.

There is no one I trust more to know the path to a *Fantastic Life* than Craig. In this book you will learn how to carve out your own goals to achieve the life you want. It's not an easy path, but with a teacher like Craig, I'm confident anyone can be Fantastic.

— Dan Sullivan
President and Co-Founder of The Strategic Coach®

Introduction

Professionally, I've helped build Lee & Associates to be one of the largest and most successful commercial real estate brokerage companies in Arizona; invested in many successful businesses; bought and sold millions of dollars of real estate; and made a good amount of money.

Personally, I've run over eighty marathons and ultra-marathons; played professional baseball in the Minnesota Twins organization; won a world championship in Tae Kwon Do; hiked around the world; completed the Marathon des Sables; earned a third degree black belt in Tae Kwon Do; and served thousands of hours with various charities like the United Way.

Most important, I've been blessed with an awesome family. We have fun together, work hard together, and love each other deeply.

My life is Fantastic.

To some, this could come off as arrogant. I don't mean it to be so. I'd be the first to admit that I don't have a *Fantastic Life* all on my own. There have been many people who have contributed to it. But it'd be dishonest to say that I had nothing to do with building it.

As with anything, building a *Fantastic Life* is a combination of deep planning, hard work, good fortune, determination, and great guidance—all of which I've had in spades. Now, as I get older and my kids are getting ready to finish college, I find a great desire to sit down and articulate to them what I've learned over the last few decades. In short, I want my kids to have a *Fantastic Life* like mine. So, this book is my loving attempt to record the rules that have helped me achieve a *Fantastic Life*. I want to impart some of the wisdom that was passed on to me as I grew up and that which I've learned on my own— sometimes the wrong way. But the good news is that the rules I lay out in this book are universal rules that will be helpful for anyone. I write them for my kids' benefit, but I hope you'll benefit from them as well.

Discovering the *Fantastic Life*

What is your *Fantastic Life*?

Is it to get a better job? Make more money? Have more time for your family? Be in better shape? Write a book? Finish reading a book? Because we're all individuals, and because there are millions of worthy and amazing things to do and accomplish in life, we all have a different definition of what the *Fantastic Life* is. This book is not about defining for you what that life is. Instead, it's about helping you discover whatever it is for you and getting you to the finish line. In the following chapters, I share eighteen rules that I've learned over the decades on what it takes to define and achieve your *Fantastic Life*.

If you're reading this book, there's a good chance that you want to see your life improve in some way. You most likely saw the words "*Fantastic Life*" in the title and were drawn to the possibilities of what that could be. It doesn't matter if your life is a total disaster, or if you're looking to find a couple new insights into making a good life even better. The rules in this book can help you discover and live your *Fantastic Life*.

And that brings us to the other reality, you probably saw the word, "Rules," and cringed. No one likes rules, but they're essential for everything in life. Rules are around for a reason, and generally for our own good. It's when we break the rules that things most often go wrong in our lives. For instance, we all know how dangerous texting and driving is, but that doesn't stop people from doing it. Unfortunately, there are serious consequences associated with breaking rules like that, so we must be careful to learn and stick to them to keep us on the right path.

The reality is that anyone can live a *Fantastic Life*, but not everyone will. Why? A number of factors; sometimes they are external, but almost always they are internal. And it's the internal reasons that are the most disappointing.

Generally, we're our own worst enemy. The default mode of most people is to pass the buck. When things are not going the way we want them to in life, we look for someone or something to blame. Occasionally, there really is someone or something holding us back, but most of the time, we're the only ones to blame. The rules in this book are not complicated, but they are hard. They require discipline and determination. They will challenge you to change the way you've been living and to try new things. They will ask you to adapt and adjust—but for the better. If you commit to them, they will reward you.

Getting real

The first step in living a *Fantastic Life* is to have an honest talk with yourself about where your life is now—to shoot straight about where you're at and how you're living. No one likes doing that, but it's key. And sometimes, well, most of the time, it's sobering.

I'm continually taking stock of myself. Years ago, my life was consumed by my work—something I have a tendency to do even today. I was trying to build my brokerage business into a large and successful company. While the company was doing well and making good money, my work felt rushed and repetitive. On top of that, I was exhausted, working long hours, seven days a week, and taking no vacations. I was involved in every aspect of every transaction, and it was killing me. Working excessively prevented me from giving the time and attention that I wanted to give, and that was needed, to my young family and my other interests. I was on the road to total burnout. I needed help.

Fortunately, help came in the form of a fellow entrepreneur I met who seemed to be able to balance the demands of running a company with the joys of living a great life. Curious, I asked what the secret was.

"I have a great coach!" he said.

Knowing that this guy was the kind of man I wanted to be around, I enrolled into his coaching program and began a course to a new way of living. That coaching program gave me a path that guides my life today.

The first thing I did those many years ago was to sit down and ask a very simple but profound question, "What is *my Fantastic Life?*" I had ideas of what the *Fantastic Life* might be from movies, friends' lives, and what I'd been told and taught, but I'd never actually sat down and thoughtfully discovered what the *Fantastic Life* meant for me.

At the time, I wrote down these goals:

- Achieve financial independence.

- Slow down, focus, and work from a plan.

- Diversify my business.

- Do a variety of different things—in my work and in my spare time.

- Spend more time with my wife and family.

- Commit to my community.

It wasn't just enough to envision my goals, however. From there, I had to develop a plan to accomplish these things. It wasn't just about the end results, it was about the process that would get me there. The steps in my plan had to be very specific to get me where I wanted:

- Adding skilled members to my business team, which would allow me to concentrate on the key parts of a transaction I was best at, like negotiations and relationship-building, and hand off the other 70 percent.

- Diversifying from one company to multiple companies and becoming an angel investor.

- Broadening my horizons by spending time with my wife and children and traveling as a family.

- Starting to do charitable work.

The results of this planning were amazing:

- My income multiplied ten times—though I expended less effort to produce it.

- I built a business that was not just successful, but consistently successful.

- I earned the top three designations in the real estate industry: CCIM, CRE, and SIOR—making me one of only thirty-five people worldwide to do so.

- I helped my real estate company grow to be one of the largest and most respected in Arizona.

- I invested in twenty different companies and helped to run four of them.

- I devoted an average of 1,000 hours a year to charities like United Way.

- I took six to eight weeks of trips with my wife and family each year, and was always present for my children's events.

It was a vast departure from where I was, but it didn't happen by accident and didn't happen overnight. I had to change my way of thinking and develop a new mindset for the way in which I tackled life, and it all started with me defining what my *Fantastic Life* was.

The *Fantastic Life* evolves

Once I started achieving my initial goals, the most curious thing happened; I started feeling restless. "How could this happen?" I wondered. Wasn't I on the road to achieving everything that I'd set out to do in building my *Fantastic Life*? The answer was yes, but the lesson was this: the *Fantastic Life* isn't static. It's not a destination that once achieved is checked off a to-do list. No, the *Fantastic Life* is a state of mind and a continuous process.

What does that mean? It means that the things you want to focus on and accomplish in life, what you consider success, will change. But what must not change, what is essential, is having a state of mind that allows you to always live a *Fantastic Life*, whatever that means to you at the time.

My *Fantastic Life* today looks different than it did when I first began my journey. Today, I'm focused on being a great husband, the best dad I can be, building my businesses, being the best athlete I can be and taking care of my body, and excelling at community service. I want each one of these areas to be exemplary, and when I'm hitting on all cylinders, I'm living my *Fantastic Life*.

Can you follow the rules?

Over the years, as I've pursued my *Fantastic Life*, I've developed my eighteen rules for living the *Fantastic Life* that I'm finally ready to share in this book. These are my guiding principles. Some of them I've developed myself. Others, I've learned from wise men and women. All of them, if followed, will allow anyone to live a *Fantastic Life*.

"If followed" is the key, however. You can live the *Fantastic Life*. I've no doubt about it. But it's all on you. At the end of the day, if you're not following these rules, and as a result, not living the life you want to live, you are responsible.

How do I know this? Because I'm not some guru offering up hollow advice that I've never used. Rather, these are battle-worn rules that I've applied in my life for success and seen others do the same. I've been there, I've done that, and I'm still doing it.

And now it's your turn. Let's get started with Rule #1: Know Your Story.

Rule #1
Know Your Story

The Dash
by Linda Ellis

I read of a man who stood to speak
at the funeral of a friend.
He referred to the dates on her tombstone,
from the beginning…to the end.

He noted that first came the date of her birth
and spoke of the following date with tears,
but he said what mattered most of all
was the dash between those years.

For that dash represents all the time
that she spent alive on earth.
And now only those who loved her
know what that little line is worth.

For it matters not, how much we own,
the cars…the house…the cash.
What matters is how we live and love
and how we spend our dash.

So, think about this long and hard.
Are there things you'd like to change?
For you never know how much time is left
that can still be rearranged.

If we could just slow down enough
to consider what's true and real
and always try to understand
the way other people feel.

And be less quick to anger
and show appreciation more
and love the people in our lives
like we've never loved before.

If we treat each other with respect
and more often wear a smile,
remembering that this special dash
might only last a little while.

So, when your eulogy is being read,
with your life's actions to rehash…
would you be proud of the things they say
about how you spent YOUR dash?

Reprinted With Permission. "The Dash" by Linda Ellis. Copyright 1996 Linda Ellis. www.lindaellis.net

Write your own epitaph?

The Dash is a critical look at the old saying, "Write your own epitaph." I've never been a fan of this sentiment. Why? Because in the scope of life, it matters little what your epitaph says. What does matter is that *you* live the life you desire. When the end of your life comes, you don't want to look back filled with regret that you didn't live it to the max. And you don't want to lament all the things that deep down inside you wanted to accomplish but never had the courage to begin. Rather than say, "Write your own epitaph," I like to say, "What is your story?"

We all have two stories

Bernie Madoff had two stories.

The story Bernie told everyone was that he was a successful financial advisor that could make you rich with his knowledge of money and markets. Over the course of his career, Bernie convinced some of the richest people in the world of this story, fooling them into handing over billions in holdings for him to manage.

The true story of Bernie Madoff was one of a crook. Bernie lost his investors over $18 billion dollars in wealth when his Ponzi scheme came crashing down—the biggest financial fraud in U.S. history. Now he'll spend the rest of his days in prison, penniless and reviled (*New York* magazine famously portrayed him as the Joker on their cover, with the headline, "Bernie Madoff, Monster"), bringing shame to himself and his family.

Though an extreme example, Bernie's story is a cautionary tale for us all. Each of us has two stories: the story we tell others and the story we know deep down in our heart. The question is, are those two stories the same? Many times they are not.

What do you want your story to be?

So, what's your story? Even more important, is it the story you want it to be?

These are fundamental questions we must ask ourselves if we want to live a *Fantastic Life*. Finding the answers takes the integrity and honesty to look into ourselves, understand what we want from life, and truthfully examine if our actions are reflecting our inner story—or if we're living one story but believing another. In the end, it's essential that our actions speak louder than our words. People should be able to look at our lives and know that we are living the stories we're telling. If you do that, you don't have to write your own epitaph. It will be visible to everyone each day of your life.

This is not a comfortable thing to do, but it is necessary and healthy. If you find that you're not living the story you want to, it takes courage and fortitude to admit that and begin living your true, inner story.

You be you

Compounding the tragedy of living conflicting stories is the fact that there are many people who will want to write our story for us. These people may be well-intentioned and want good things for us that may not fit in with our true story. Or they may be roadblocks, forcing a story on us that we do not want. This was demonstrated for me in a powerful way many years ago as I was running the Marathon des Sables.

The Marathon des Sables is one of the hardest things I've ever done in my life. It's a 150-mile, self-supported race in the Sahara. They give you nine liters of water a day. That's it. You carry all your food and all your safety equipment. You're on your own, and there's no trail. Much like the Tour de France, the race is run in stages over seven days. There's a marathon stage, a dune day where it's a hundred percent dunes, a fifty-mile stage, and others.

I went with Paul, a friend of mine who's done a bunch of long-distance running with me, and the night before the fifty-mile stage—the make-or-break stage—he got dysentery. In the desert, if you get diarrhea, you're done. He had to drop out at mile five, and I still had forty-five miles to go that day!

I ran all day by myself. Then in the evening, as the sun was setting, I was at a water station and met up with another runner named John. Together we ran into the dark, knowing we had five to seven hours to go until the end of the stage.

As we went along, we started chatting. It was a beautiful night with the most amazing stars out. We were in the middle of nowhere in Morocco in the Sahara—quite a setting. I asked him, "Tell me, what's your story? Why are you here?" His answer demonstrated the importance of living your own story.

"All my life my dad told me I'd never be anybody," he said. "When I was eighteen-years old, I left home. My dad said, 'You're lazy, and you'll never amount to anything.' So, I joined the Navy. Now I teach swimming to Navy enlistees. To train for the marathon, every day I'd get to the pool in the early hours before work and run around the pool for two hours wearing 50-pounds of firefighter gear. The gear doesn't breathe. It feels like 160 degrees in there. I pushed my body to the extreme at every opportunity. That's how I trained for this."

As he told me the story of his dad, I asked, "Do you talk to your dad? Does he even know you're here?"

"I didn't tell him until the night before I left," John said. "I called my dad and said, 'Dad, this is John. I want to let you know I'm leaving tomorrow morning, and I'm going to run the Marathon des Sables…and I'm going to finish.' And then I hung up the phone. I didn't let him reply."

His story made me pause. Here was a guy whose entire life was driven from the fact that his dad told him he'd never be anything. He had a choice to live the story that his dad had told him about himself…or to make his own story.

At that point, I knew two things: 1) John was going to finish the fifty-mile leg, and 2) I had picked the right guy to run with through the night. He finished that race, an incredible achievement. But the bigger achievement for John was writing his own story. He knew what he wanted in life, and he trained hard to achieve it.

Chances are, you're like John. There are many people in life trying to tell you who you are, what your story is, and what you should want in life. Today, you have a choice—be yourself or be what others tell you to be. Which will it be?

If you want to write your own story, the first step is being crystal clear on what you want. And that's what we'll talk about next.

Action items

1   Set aside some time to determine what you want your story to be.

2   Honestly examine whether you're living your story or living some other story.

3. If you're living another story, determine today what it will take to start living your true story. Formulate a plan to live your true story and start living it.

Remind yourself each day of the story you want to live and do everything in your power to live in such a way that is true to your story.

Helpful questions to ask

1. What do I want my story to be at the end of my life? Am I living in a way that honors that story and are my actions in accordance with my story?

2. What parts of my story are the parts I want and what parts are those that others have defined for me?

3. What actions do I need to take to begin living in alignment with my true story?

Rule #2
Be Crystal Clear On What You Want

When several other guys and I started Lee & Associates, life was very busy. The demands of my work were high, and I found that balancing my role as a great husband and new dad, pursuing activities I was passionate about, and building a successful company were incredibly challenging.

Before long, it was clear that my work was taking over my life. I found myself working *in* my business rather than working *on* it. I was still building my career, running with every deal that came my way, and working on everything from the smallest decisions to the broad strategic planning. The result? Long hours, lack of sleep, and very little time with my family. I was exhausted, getting up at three o'clock in the morning to head into the office six days a week.

Sometimes, I would even fall asleep while driving! This continued for fifteen years. I knew I could not keep this pace forever. It was time to reorient my priorities. The hard part was getting to that point.

Some people, when they find themselves in this cycle, will respond by sacrificing everything for one thing. Others will double down, try to do everything well and, in the process, do nothing well. Others will simply tap out and quit. None of those were options I found acceptable.

Instead, I took a step back and took inventory. Was there a way I could succeed at the things I valued most in life: my family, hobbies, and work? I found that it was possible, but it would take intentionality and a plan. And I needed some help.

Thankfully, I found that help in the form of coaching by Dan Sullivan, creator of the Strategic Coach® Program. Dan helped me, and still helps me, examine my life as it was and as I wanted it to be. In his program, I developed a winning plan that paved the way for a balanced and healthy life. I made a few things a priority, discarded unimportant things, and created a road map to success.

It all started with being crystal clear on what I wanted and understanding my Unique Ability®.

Examine your life

Living a *Fantastic Life* takes honesty. The first step in knowing what you want in life is to take stock of your life as it is. Most people don't like to examine their lives too carefully because they're scared of what they'll find.

For instance, my friend Joe wanted to be the top real estate agent in his city. He did well for himself, but he found that he wasn't nearly reaching the deal flow that he wanted. For years, he thought that the cards would land his way, but they never did. He was working hard and putting in long days, but he never stopped to take a look at what those days really entailed. Once he did, he saw a pattern of unhealthy behavior that was hampering his growth.

Joe needed to redefine what it meant to work hard. He took care of listings that came his way, but did not focus on expanding his business. For him, an eight- to ten-hour day seemed like a lot, but, like I did early in my life, he was really working *in* his business, not *on* it. What's more, after the workday, he often found himself at the bar having a few drinks with buddies. A few drinks turned into a few more, and a handful of nights a month turned into every other day.

Once Joe got the courage to examine his life honestly, he found himself in the throws of alcohol dependency. Excessive drinking handicapped his ability to create the life he wanted. Rather than use his "off" hours to grow professionally, he drank. By the time he was aware of how much time he had squandered in bars, he came to an even scarier realization—Joe was an alcoholic. And unless he addressed this issue, he'd never get ahead. Joe joined AA.

Fast-forward and Joe is now sober. Through the process of examining his behaviors and making key changes, he's radically altered his life. Instead of hitting the bars after showing properties, Joe began to network and study his business. Instead of being too tired at night to do a bit of extra work, he found new energy he didn't know he possessed, that he used to pursue new listings and expand his business. Instead of being out too much, Joe found himself present, laughing and enjoying time with his wife and kids. Today, twenty years later, he is one of the top agents in Phoenix. Joe is a community leader, a great dad, and a wonderful guy—and it all started with examining his life.

How about you? What does your life look like? Have you ever stopped to take stock and see how you're allocating your time and energy towards the most important things in your life? It may seem like a scary thing to do, but if you want to live the *Fantastic Life*, it is essential. Do it today.

Set your priorities

Another friend of mine, Jake, is a successful writer. When he was in his mid-twenties, Jake was working three jobs. He was acquiring apartment buildings for a local investment company during the day, working as a lay pastor on the weekends for his church, and trying to build a freelance writing business in the evenings and mornings.

Jake quickly found himself putting in 80 to 100 hours a week. In the process his family was suffering. He also found himself skipping meals and workouts, and his health was declining. A wake-up moment for Jake was when his lower back gave out after years of sitting hunched over a desk without any activity to counterbalance it. As he spent months rehabilitating, he was faced with a decision to keep going down his destructive path or to make some big changes.

Knowing things had to change, Jake took inventory of his life and realized that he was trying to make everything a priority and doing nothing with a plan. The result was that he was doing well at one or two things but failing miserably at most others. He decided it was time to set his priorities.

For Jake, this meant choosing what was most important in his life and throwing all his energy at those things. He determined his priorities were God, family, health, and writing. This meant making some hard decisions. He quit his lucrative and promising acquisition job, focused on his freelance work, and used his off time to volunteer at the church, work out, and spend quality time with his family.

This also meant that Jake had to be extremely disciplined with his time. He set up a rigid schedule: getting up at five o'clock in the morning to write; using the afternoons to source more work for his writing business; hitting the gym after that; spending the evenings at the dinner table engaged with his family and playing with his kids afterwards; planning dates with his wife; doing a bit more work in the evenings before bed; and participating in church activities on the weekend. He found this also meant cutting out many of the social activities he did with friends. He simply didn't have the time. It was a small price to pay to pursue his priorities.

Jake found that by determining his priorities in life, every decision on what and what not to do became easier for him. He had a plan. Today, Jake has worked on over seventeen books with clients, writes frequently for the web, and is a partner in a creative agency. His life is radically different than it was ten years ago, and he'll tell you it all goes back to setting his priorities in his twenties.

How about you? Is your life overwhelmed with activities that aren't necessarily important to you but that are taking up a majority of your time? Are you finding you have a desire to do something but are unable to accomplish it? The solution could be as simple as setting your priorities and pursuing them above everything else. Today is the day to set your priorities.

You can have anything… but not everything

Both Joe and Jake learned a valuable lesson in examining their lives and setting their priorities: you can have anything in life…but not everything. As humans, we only have so much capacity to accomplish things. And as the old saying goes, "There are only 24 hours in a day."

All this is to say that a fundamental principle of living a *Fantastic Life* is to acknowledge that there will always be constraints. The good news is that constraints are helpful.

The best work is done in the context of constraints. For instance, my best clients are those who know what they want *and* what their constraints are. The money they're looking to spend, the business they conduct, the area they want to be in…these are all constraints that help me find the perfect fit for them. My clients could pursue anything they want in a property, but they can't pursue everything they want. For instance, they can't have a top-floor office in one of the nicest buildings in town and still pay affordable rates. It's not possible. But they can probably choose one of the two.

In life, it's the same for us. It's all about understanding that pursuing what we really want will take some sacrifice—and we must be okay with those sacrifices.

Make a list

If you're ready to examine your life, the best thing you can do is start by making a list. Personally, I think it's best to look at everything in your life and write down the top five things you want. I call these my résumés, and we'll study that concept in the next chapter.

Once you create a list of your top five priorities, you need to examine everything that keeps you from focusing on those priorities. Then comes the hard part: anything that holds you back, cut out of your life. That could be anything from nights out with friends to your job. The point is to identify them, list them, and know them.

Filter your life

The final step in this process is to the use your top five priorities as the filter for every decision and action you take in life. If creating a side business is a priority, then you might sacrifice nights out with friends for time with your family. If you want to focus on your family, but you have a great idea for a side project, you need to shelve the idea for later when life affords time to focus on it. Whatever you do in life, you must look at it through your priority filter and act accordingly.

Once you cut out the extra things, it's time to focus fully on your priorities. I call this building your résumés, which is what we'll talk about next.

Action items

1. Stop and take inventory of your life. List all the activities you're involved in from work to home.

2. Determine your top five priorities out of the list you've developed.

3. Make a plan on how you'll focus on those priorities and another plan to remove yourself from the activities that don't make your top five list.

4. Begin filtering every decision you make on how you'll spend your time and energy through the top five things that are most important for you. Use that as the way in which you'll decide to commit to something or not.

Some helpful questions

1. What's most important to me at this period of my life?

2. Where am I really spending my time and energy? Is it on what's most important to me or on other things? Why?

3. What are the activities and commitments I'm involved in that are keeping me from focusing on my top five priorities? Why am I committing so much time to them?

4. How will I begin to cut back on things that aren't a priority to focus on those things that are?

Rule #3
Build Your Résumé Every Year

If you look up the word "résumé" on Google, you'll find over 500 million hits. There are all sorts of articles on building your résumé getting your résumé noticed, and what not to do on your résumé.

Often, when I'm talking to people, they'll say a job they didn't like was a "good résumé builder." People looking for work spend weeks perfecting their résumé. Many people flaunt their résumé. In a lot of ways your résumé is one of the most important documents in life. It's a big deal.

At the end of the day, your résumé is a list of accomplishments. When we build a work résumé, we list the positions we've held at various companies, the training we have for our jobs, and awards and recognitions related to our career path. A good résumé is one that demonstrates that you're accomplished and skilled enough to work in an available position—whether or not you're a potential asset to the company. Hiring managers are notorious for looking at a résumé in a few seconds and knowing whether to toss it aside or put it into a stack for further consideration. Your résumé has to be concise, informative, organized, and impressive. Otherwise you're collecting unemployment checks.

Treat life like your work

If a résumé is so important, if we spend so much time and energy on building and perfecting our résumé, shouldn't that same energy and passion go into building and perfecting the *Fantastic Life*?

Many years ago, I began creating résumés for every area of my life. While I still put tremendous amounts of effort into my work résumé, I also apply that same commitment to other aspects of my life.

In treating my life résumés like my work résumé, I acknowledge the fact that all of life is connected. Too often we compartmentalize our lives. We apply ourselves at work and slack off everywhere else because we think no one is watching. But if you're not disciplined and working to grow personally, emotionally, and physically, you'll find yourself failing at work, too.

I've always believed that if you're going to do something, you need to do it all the way. Otherwise, don't do it at all. By treating all of life like I treat work, I focus on building résumés in important areas that help me to be the best that I can be—at work, at home, and everywhere else I find myself.

Build five résumés per year

At the end of the year, people often sit down and review their work résumé. In doing so, they analyze what was accomplished over the course of twelve months. In what areas did you grow? Did you accomplish your goals? What can be updated to make the résumé more comprehensive and impressive?

I do the same thing each year, too, but I do it with more than just work. I sit down and determine the five most important things I want to focus on, and I either create or review my résumé for each area.

For instance, athletics are very important to me. I played professional baseball when I was younger. I'm a runner, participating in many marathons. I even own part of a company that specializes in athletic movement. For me, it's very important that I grow as an athlete. This means there are certain years I'll focus heavily on building my sports résumé with very specific goals.

I did this several years back when I decided I wanted to become a black belt in Martial Arts.

After I researched different types of Martial Arts, I visited five different Dojos. I decided to focus on Tae Kwon Do, and through intense training over the next three years, I obtained my black belt. I had reached my goal, but still desired to attain certain skills. So, I reset my goals. After three more years of hard work, I earned a second degree. Four years later, I earned my third degree. At that point, I had the skills and the confidence I committed to, all those years before. In 2004, I was a member of the World Champion United States Tae Kwon Do Team, winning two gold medals and an overall team championship in the South Korea games.

For me, Tae Kwon Do is now a significant part of my athletic résumé, just one aspect of a long list of athletic accomplishments in my life that I can always return to, review, and build on. My athletic résumé looks like this:

My love for athletics started as a child. From a young age, I had a ball and glove in hand. My dad was the hometown baseball coach and is now in the Coaches Hall of Fame. I was an All-Star player in high school, coached for NuttyBuddy, set three school records at Nicholls State University, earned a Lifetime Membership from the Association of Professional Baseball Players, made All-Conference at Yavapai College, and was drafted in 1983 as a professional baseball player with the Minnesota Twins.

I have run over eighty marathons, including the Western States 100, Marathon des Sables (152-mile trek in the Sahara Desert), Boston Marathon, New York Marathon, Los Angeles Marathon, and countless more. And to date, I am still an ultra-hiker, spending twenty nights a year on the ground.

Each year, I create five different résumés. I find that this is the perfect number. If I try for any more, I set myself up to fail by focusing on too much. If I make progress in each of my five résumés, I feel a strong sense of accomplishment, but some years my growth is small (or even negative). Progress does not come in a linear fashion. The point is to understand what the next step is in building your résumé. It all goes back to rule #2 of the *Fantastic Life*: being clear on what you want in life and focusing on those things.

My five résumés are:

Husband

I want to be a great husband. When I look at my husband résumé, I want to see that I'm growing in the way I love my wife. Do I have a deeper relationship with her? Am I connecting more than I was a year ago? What can I do this year to build my relationship and make it better?

Father

A lot of people lump family together. For me, it's important to separate out my family résumé into husband and father. They are very different relationships that require very different types of focused work and growth. I like to sit down and review my relationship with each of my kids. Are they growing? Is my relationship with them evolving? How can I be a better dad and help them be the best people they can be? What has changed in my kids' lives that require me to change the way I approach and interact with them?

Business

Are my businesses growing? Where am I with each business? What is the next step? Did I improve areas of my business that needed working on in the last year?

Athlete

Is my athletic résumé better? Did I complete events? Have I set any personal records? Accomplished any significant achievements? At fifty-one years old I still consider myself an athlete. For instance, this year I solo-hiked the Alt Via in Italy, a 125-mile hike across the Dolomites. I added that to my athletic résumé.

Personal Growth

Am I working more in my Unique Ability®? Have I grown as a person? What additional education have I finished? Is my spiritual life growing?

Your résumés will be different, unique to your experience and goals. The point is that you must not only identify what's important in your life, you must also work on building your résumés in those areas, always striving to improve each year.

Life is not a destination

I find that building résumés helps me stay motivated. There's something refreshing about being able to look back at all that I've accomplished over the years. While it's important to have goals, it's just as important to see that you've been able to accomplish them. Reviewing your résumé makes things that initially seem insurmountable seem doable in perspective. My résumés can serve as a shot in the arm when I need to keep moving forward and growing.

As the saying goes, "If you're not growing, you're dying." Perhaps most important to remember when building your résumés is that there is no stopping point. There's never a time when I sit down to review my résumés and say, "That's it. I've accomplished all I can. Everything is perfect." Rather, I understand that my résumés reflect a mindset, not prescribe a destination. They remind me of where I've been and that I must keep moving forward.

You'd never want your work résumé to sit stagnant. The same goes for your life résumés. You should always be evaluating where you can grow. Doing this gives your life purpose and keeps you moving forward. It makes you a better person and allows you to accomplish things you've never dreamed of over the course of time.

Action Items

1. Determine your top five priorities in life.

2. Create a résumé for each with accomplishments from the past and goals for the coming year.

3. Sit down each year to review your résumés, update them, and determine what progress you can make on each résumé you'll be working on. Keep in mind that life changes; some years your progress will be nominal and other years massive. The goal is progress.

Some helpful questions to ask

1. What's most important to me in life? Am I focusing on those or did I let other things crowd in and distract me?

2. What are the most important things I want to accomplish? Are those realistic goals? Don't set yourself up for failure.

3. What significant achievements have I had in the last year? Did I accomplish all that I set out to do? If so, why? If not, why?

Rule #4
All of Life is Connected

At 3:32 p.m. on August 14, 2003, an overheating electrical line sagged onto a tree just outside the city of Cleveland, Ohio. As a result, a huge amount of strain was put on other electrical lines in the state. Soon, the utility that served Southern Ohio sealed itself off as its lines burned under the pressure of the one failing line. This created an electrical barrier between the southern part of the state and the northern part of the state.

Without power from the southern power station, the city of Cleveland was starved for electricity. As a result they drew power from Michigan and Ontario, which knocked out more power lines and power plants. This started a chain reaction, causing power plants in northwestern New York to malfunction.

In reaction, New York sealed off its power plants, cutting power off from Canada. This created a different problem. With nowhere to send the extra electricity created, the New York plants overloaded their system. This forced the plants to shut down completely.

The result? The largest blackout in the history of the United States, cutting off power in eight states and leaving tens of millions without power.

Isn't it amazing that the largest blackout in U.S. history was a culmination of very small events? One malfunctioning power line shut down power for millions.

This serves to illustrate a very important and often overlooked fact: the most complex things are often the most fragile. Why? Because complex systems rely on connections. The more connections there are, the greater the chance that one connection can break, sending the whole system crashing. This is why billions of dollars are spent to analyze, protect, and failsafe systems.

Life is complicated

If you think that an electrical grid is complex, think about your life.

Each day you rely on thousands of external connections. You rely on electricity for your alarm clock to go off, to turn on the lights so you can see, to cook your breakfast, power your phone, and more. You rely on the Internet and communication grids to access important information for your work and to stay connected to loved ones. You rely on your kids to get ready for school so that you can be on time for work. You rely on oil production companies to get crude oil to refineries to make into gasoline so you can fuel your car to get where you need to go. You rely on your co-workers and employees to show up and do their job so that you can do yours. The list goes on and on.

The simple truth is this: all of life is connected, and life is complicated.

Take control

In life, each decision we make, each activity we participate in, each interaction we have, are all connected to one another. There is always a cause and always an effect. That's why priorities are so important.

For instance, many marriages end because of money problems. But is it really that simple? Think about the things that happen when money becomes a problem. Some people try to buckle down and work more to make up for the shortfalls. The extra time in the office can often result in less time at home. This puts a strain on a marriage, and if you have kids, the stress is broader. The kids might start acting out in negative ways, causing more stress in the home and more tension in the marriage. The stress can also lead to substance abuse, which can put a tremendous burden on a relationship. The point is that an imbalance in one part of life can lead to many more imbalances. Just like the power stations in the Northeast, things can quickly become overloaded, and soon you're looking at a complete meltdown.

The same applies to your health. If you don't take care of your body or you do things that are harmful, like smoking, you'll face health problems. This can cause problems at work. As a result, you'll face money problems, both in the form of increased medical costs and lost income from your job. This leads to stress that can impact your family and emotional health. It's all connected.

Because all of life is connected, you must make sure to take control of every area of your life if you want to live a *Fantastic Life*. Many people lead unbalanced lives. Partly, this is because some areas of life come more naturally than others. Some men, for instance, often find it easier to focus on work than on being a husband and a dad. Rather than do the hard work of excelling both at home and at work, they'll focus on work, and the family will suffer. Likewise, people who struggle with weight issues may actually like to exercise but never gain any traction because they can't control how they eat.

The key to living the *Fantastic Life* is to understand that everything is connected, and therefore you must give your full effort to the things that are most important to you. This means that, like we've talked about before, you must establish your priorities and understand that focusing on your priorities will have consequences for other areas of your life—and you must be okay with those consequences.

Don't be afraid to ask for help

Part of taking control of your life and making sure you are at peak performance is knowing your weaknesses, and being ready to ask for help.

For example, those people who have money problems need help from those who understand money; those who struggle with weight need a trainer; marriages that are crumbling need counselors; and those struggling with substance abuse need programs.

For me, I struggled with saying "No." That's why I sought help from a life coach to help me establish my priorities and make a plan for taking control of my life, rather than be controlled by the messes created by trying to do too much. I wasn't afraid to ask for help, and you shouldn't be either.

Enjoy the benefits

You may fear what you'll find when you dig this deep into your life. It's scary to see all the areas where you don't have control. But even scarier is not doing anything at all and watching helplessly as things break down. Failure is always a part of life, but the worst kind of failure is the failure that comes from doing nothing. It's always preferable to fail while trying.

But more likely, you'll find that as you grow in living a focused life, your life will be much better than it was before. Sure, there'll be an initial period of pain and growth, but nothing worthwhile comes pain-free. The good news is that once you understand that all of life is

Don't be afraid to ask for help

Part of taking control of your life and making sure you are at peak performance is knowing your weaknesses, and being ready to ask for help.

For example, those people who have money problems need help from those who understand money; those who struggle with weight need a trainer; marriages that are crumbling need counselors; and those struggling with substance abuse need programs.

For me, I struggled with saying "No." That's why I sought help from a life coach to help me establish my priorities and make a plan for taking control of my life, rather than be controlled by the messes created by trying to do too much. I wasn't afraid to ask for help, and you shouldn't be either.

Enjoy the benefits

You may fear what you'll find when you dig this deep into your life. It's scary to see all the areas where you don't have control. But even scarier is not doing anything at all and watching helplessly as things break down. Failure is always a part of life, but the worst kind of failure is the failure that comes from doing nothing. It's always preferable to fail while trying.

But more likely, you'll find that as you grow in living a focused life, your life will be much better than it was before. Sure, there'll be an initial period of pain and growth, but nothing worthwhile comes pain-free. The good news is that once you understand that all of life is connected, and do all you can to make sure every area of your life is focused and prioritized, you'll enjoy tremendous benefit from it—and so will those whom you love.

Lack of focus isn't a one-time problem

As a final word, it's important to understand that just like power grids are always monitored, life doesn't stay in focus automatically, even when we've worked hard to get to a good point. There are all sorts of things that will ultimately create a lack of focus in life like financial crisis, health issues, and more.

Like all of life, the process of finding focus is one that is continual and fluid. It's a mindset, not a destination. Understanding that fact will allow you to both have grace for yourself and others, and stay vigilant in always examining your life and actively taking control of it. I've done this and do it every day. And so can you.

Start finding focus today.

Action items

1. Take stock of your life and figure out where you may be out of focus.

2. Ask people that you trust in your life where they see you living out of focus. Compare their lists with yours.

3. Make an action plan to find focus.

4. Seek help from professionals where needed.

Rule #5
Make Sacrifices

Lily had always been very social. As a young girl she hosted tea parties, keeping a captive audience of dolls, teddy bears, and her obliging younger sister. Noticing her aptitude for entertaining and her gift of gab, her parents enrolled her in dance and drama classes. Lily was a natural on the stage. Dance instructors and casting directors took notice and before long Lily landed leading roles at the local theater company.

Lily immersed herself in acting. She attended workshops, took private classes, and auditioned for anything and everything that came along. When Lily graduated from high school, she had two options: go to college or move to the Big Apple and pursue her real dream…Broadway. Although Lily's friends and family had always embraced and encouraged her love for acting, when it came time to choose between an education and a life on the stage, her parents were adamant about the importance of going to school to one day get a "real job."

Lily was a very, very good student. She earned straight A's through school, participated in honors programs, and had a real gift for writing. But her real love, acting, tugged at her heart even as she sat through her SATs and filled out college applications. Conventional wisdom told her to take the traditional path: college, then career. That path became harder to ignore as the acceptance letters poured in from the top schools across the country. Lily found herself in a hard spot. She spent most of her life meeting or exceeding other people's expectations—her parents', her teachers', and her audiences'. Rarely, if ever, did Lily say, "No," whether to a role or an academic activity.

At 18 years old, Lily had a tough choice ahead of her. She had to say "No" to something. Would Lily defy her parents' wishes, pack her belongs into a bag, and head to New York City to chase after her passion? Or would she take the safer, more secure path, and spend four years at an Ivy League school, get a solid degree, and find a worthwhile career?

Lily decided to take a risk. She said, "No," for the first time, knowing she was making a tremendous sacrifice. Broadway wasn't a sure thing, and the choice came with lots of questions: Would she land a role? Would she have to work three jobs? Would she even be able to pay her rent? Despite the unknowns (and after a Valedictorian speech at high school graduation about audacity and dreams and sacrifice), Lily loaded her car with the necessities and headed East for the city.

The *Fantastic Life* requires sacrifice

The point of Lily's story is that everything in life requires sacrifice. The decisions we make, whether for good or for bad, all have downsides. The question is, what are you willing to sacrifice?

Now that you've determined what's most important to you in life, you need to be willing to make the sacrifices required to accomplish those important things. There are downsides to every decision. The goal should not be to avoid sacrifice: rather it should be to make the right sacrifices. Remember, you can have anything you want in life, but you can't have everything.

Most people aren't proactive when it comes to sacrifice. They instead let life lead them by the nose with little thought as to what the end will be. Lily bucked this convention. Pursuing her *Fantastic Life* meant taking a risk and making the hard decision. Even as a young woman, she chose to do what it takes to achieve her priorities rather than simply listen to everyone else because it's easier.

For Lily, the sacrifices of a quality education and a secure career are worth the priorities of chasing her dream to live a life on the stage. She believes that the sacrifices she's making now at a young age will result in a life that will bring lasting value and hopefully little regret. This is not to say that Lily won't face hard times, but she is being proactive in making her sacrifices.

Sacrifice what holds you back

Perhaps the most important skill in making sacrifices is in being able to identify what will keep you from being successful in life. For instance, I made a decision many years ago that I didn't want to drink a lot of alcohol. It's not that I had a drinking problem, nor did I have any moral issue with it. Rather, alcohol wasn't part of my *Fantastic Life* because I knew it would detract from what was important to me. Because I want to have a good relationship with my wife and kids, be a stellar athlete, and have a winning business, I knew I couldn't afford to go out late and not be able to get up in the morning. A few fun nights out with the guys weren't worth the cost.

Now, twenty years later, my decision to sacrifice social drinking has paid off. Even if I saved only three hours a week, that's roughly 3,000 hours over the course of twenty years. To put that in perspective, that's almost two years' worth of eight-hour working days that I've gained back through my decision.

I'm not saying don't drink. What I am saying is determine what's important to you and what will hold you back from accomplishing those things. Then sacrifice those things for the greater goal. For me, not drinking was part of the sacrifice I needed to make to get where I am today. For you, it could be any number of things. With everything, you need to count the cost.

Create your reality

The practice of actively saying "No" is really the practice of creating your own reality. Those who don't actively make sacrifices instead let the world determine what should be sacrificed for them. For instance, many people lost it all during the housing crisis because they bought a house they couldn't afford and didn't need. Why would they do this? Most often it was because it was expected of them. Our culture values getting ahead of the Joneses, and many people don't stop to think if that's what's really important to them. Instead, they passively make life decisions to fit in with the pack. Other people spend years toiling away at a job they can't stand because they were taught from a young age that work and play are two different things, and that it's more important to be safe and secure than to be happy and take risks.

This is what I call "living in the Matrix," and part of getting out of the Matrix is to know that you must make sacrifices—and to determine what those sacrifices will be, rather than let others tell you and regret it. Staying out of the Matrix is what we'll talk about next.

Action items

1. Decide if you're making the right decisions given what is most valuable to you in life.

2. Determine the sacrifices that accomplishing your goals will require.

3. Adjust your sacrifices to actively take control of your life.

4. Live with the consequences and don't complain.

5. Learn to say "No."

Some helpful questions to ask

1. Am I actively making sacrifices in my life and controlling my reality, or am I letting others decide what should be sacrificed in my life?

2. What are the things in my life that I'm willing to sacrifice? What are the things that I'm not willing sacrifice?

3. What will be the long-term results of the things I've decided to sacrifice? How are those decisions affecting others in my life?

4. Are those results acceptable to me?

5. What can I say "No" to today to make sure that the sacrifices I'm making are those that I want to make?

Rule #6
Stay Out
of the Matrix

In the movie *The Matrix*, Thomas Anderson is a computer programmer who also lives a double life as the hacker Neo. In the course of his hacking, Neo finds mysterious references to the Matrix across the web. As he digs deeper, another hacker, Trinity, reaches out to him and introduces him to legendary hacker Morpheus, whom she promises can tell him about the Matrix.

Neo's life is turned upside down as government agents arrest and interrogate him after his contact with Trinity. In a dramatic chase, Neo escapes and finally meets Morpheus in a darkened room with two chairs and a table that holds a glass of water.

"I imagine," says Morpheus, "That right now you're feeling a bit like Alice tumbling down the rabbit hole."

"You could say that," says Neo.

"I can see it in your eyes. You have the look of a man who accepts what he sees because he's expecting to wake up. Ironically this is not far from the truth. Do you believe in fate, Neo?"

"No."

"Why not?" asks Morpheus.

"Because I don't like the idea that I'm not in control of my life."

"I know exactly what you mean. Let me tell you why you're here. You're here because you know something. What you know, you can't explain. But you feel it. You felt it your entire life. That there's something wrong with the world. You don't know what it is, but it's there. Like a splinter in your mind—driving you mad. It is this feeling that has brought you to me. Do you know what I'm talking about?"

"The Matrix?"

"Do you want to know what it is? The Matrix is everywhere; it is all around us. Even now, in this very room. You can see it when you look out your window, or when you turn on your television. You can feel it when you go to work, or when you go to church or when you pay your taxes. It is the world that has been pulled over your eyes to blind you from the truth."

"What truth?"

"That you are a slave, Neo. Like everyone else, you were born into bondage, born inside a prison that you cannot smell, taste, or touch. A prison for your mind. Unfortunately, no one can be told what the Matrix is. You have to see it for yourself. This is your last chance. After this, there is no turning back."

Morpheus offers Neo the choice between two pills, a red one and a blue one. If Neo takes the blue pill he wakes up in his own bed, believing whatever he wants to believe. If he takes the red pill, he will see what the Matrix is. Neo takes the red pill, and his whole world is turned upside down.

The Matrix is real

Though a sci-fi movie set in the future, *The Matrix* is a great metaphor for how we can live our lives. Like Neo, we can create a prison that we can't see, taste, or touch. Like Neo, we have a general sense that things are not as they should be, that there's something wrong with the world. And like Neo, we definitely don't like the idea that we aren't in control of our lives or living the way we want.

But deep down, I think most of us know that we are seldom in control of our lives, even in the areas where we should be. We're living in a Matrix. A prison for our minds. In the movie, the Matrix is a computer-simulated program that mimics the appearance of reality while sentient machines use the heat of sedated human bodies as an energy source. In our life, the Matrix is the web of expectations that society weaves around us.

If you think about it, there are many things you do each and every day because "that's how it's always done," or what "they" want us to do. Everyone is part of a Matrix of expectation, sometimes self-imposed, sometimes imposed by others. This is why people who are abused have a hard time escaping the cycle of abuse. They can't imagine a life that could be any different. This is why employees who have a great idea for a business can't bring themselves to quit their job and take a leap of faith. This is why people buy things they don't really want or need in order to gain acceptance from friends, families, and neighbors.

When I was younger, one Matrix I lived in was golf.

I hate golf, but everybody in my industry plays it. To me, golf is excruciating. It's four to five hours of sitting around and occasionally hitting a ball. You hang out with some guys, drink some beers, hit a hundred balls, and then drink some more beers and talk about the balls you hit. Absolutely zero interest for me.

Yet, I did it. Why?

For me, golf was a Matrix-created event. I can't stand it, but I did it because it was expected of me. Now, you might love golf. That's awesome. I hope you have the opportunity to play it often, and may all your shots be holes-in-one. I'm not knocking golf. What I am saying is that I spent years playing a game I didn't like just because it was something I thought I had to do. It was a prison.

Golf may not be your Matrix, but I'm sure if you thought for a second, it wouldn't be hard to figure out what is.

Take the red pill

In order to live the *Fantastic Life*, you have to get out of the Matrix. You have to take that red pill. It might be scary, but getting to the other side is worth it.

Each year, the one golf tournament I dreaded the most was our annual partner tournament for Lee & Associates. The first Thursday of every year, the company would do a golf outing that was all day long. At the end, we'd have a big dinner and would divvy up the company profits for the year. Now, I loved getting the money, but I hated having to play golf to get it.

For the first three or four years I played, and it drove me insane. Then, one year, it hit me: I don't have to play. I took the red pill.

For the last seventeen years, I've skipped the golf tournament and instead gone backpacking on Wednesday and spent the night sleeping on the ground. Now, that's my idea of fun. I'm away from the phones and computers. I get the chance to think about my last year and plan for the next. I wake up and hike all day on Thursday while everyone else is playing golf, and I have a blast. Later that day, I come back and have dinner with everyone. I enjoy the company of my partners and still get my money. And you know what? No one cares, except me—and in the best possible way. And that's all that matters. Turns out I played golf all those years when I didn't have to.

Your life is no different. You do things that you probably hate on the deepest level, but you do them because you think you have to. You don't. That's the Matrix. Take the red pill and be free.

When it comes to the *Fantastic Life*, there's nothing better than the freedom of knowing what you want out of life and being comfortable in your own skin. Start today.

Action items

1. List the things you're doing out of obligation or habit rather than because you want to.

2. List the reasons why you think you need to do those things.

3. Determine if those reasons are valid, or if they're Matrix-created.

4. List what you want to be doing that you aren't.

5. Figure out how to get out of the Matrix and to begin taking control of your life.

Some helpful questions to ask

1. What have I done in the last week that I felt I had to out of obligation or habit, even though I didn't want to?

2. Why did I do those things? What was there to gain?

3. Am I living a life others expect me to live or the life I want?

4. What is it I truly want in life?

5. What are the things I can stop doing now so that I can begin doing what I want?

Rule #7
Be Value Driven

On a somber Thursday, November 19, 1863, President Abraham Lincoln took the stage at the dedication of the Soldiers' National Cemetery in Gettysburg, Pennsylvania to commemorate the battle of Gettysburg, in which nearly 50,000 people lost their lives. It was on this stage that he gave what is now widely considered the greatest speech in American history, *The Gettysburg Address*:

> Four score and seven years ago our fathers brought forth on this continent a new nation, conceived in liberty, and dedicated to the proposition that all men are created equal.

> Now we are engaged in a great civil war, testing whether that nation, or any nation, so conceived and so dedicated, can long endure. We are met on

a great battle-field of that war. We have come to dedicate a portion of that field, as a final resting place for those who here gave their lives that that nation might live. It is altogether fitting and proper that we should do this.

But, in a larger sense, we cannot dedicate, we cannot consecrate, we cannot hallow this ground. The brave men, living and dead, who struggled here, have consecrated it, far above our poor power to add or detract. The world will little note, nor long remember what we say here, but it can never forget what they did here. It is for us the living, rather, to be dedicated here to the unfinished work, which they who fought here have thus far so nobly advanced. It is rather for us to be here dedicated to the great task remaining before us—that from these honored dead we take increased devotion to that cause for which they gave the last full measure of devotion—that we here highly resolve that these dead shall not have died in vain—that this nation, under God, shall have a new birth of freedom— and that government of the people, by the people, for the people, shall not perish from the earth.

Few people realize that Lincoln's address was not the keynote address for the Gettysburg ceremony. Edward Everett gave the actual keynote address, a two-hour event that preceded the President's speech. Much of Everett's speech revolved around eulogizing the dead and using political rhetoric to demonize the South. In short, Everett made his speech about politics. Today, it is largely forgotten.

In stark contrast, Lincoln's speech took three minutes to deliver and, while still honoring the dead, simply and succinctly appealed to the values for which they had fought and died. He didn't politicize the event but instead appealed to the highest values of humanity such as liberty and freedom, values for which Lincoln encouraged the living to give their lives to in "full measure of devotion," just as the men who died already had. Today, everyone knows about *The Gettysburg Address*.

Value drives behavior

We all know how Lincoln's story ends. He fought tirelessly to win the Civil War and secure freedom for slaves. And he paid the price with his life, just as the soldiers at Gettysburg did. The difference between Lincoln and Everett's speeches highlight an important truth—people will rarely give their life solely for a political cause, but they will for values that they hold dear.

I define values as the uncompromising truths that drive and direct our behavior. For Lincoln and the soldiers that died on the Gettysburg field, and in many other battles, it was values that they held as uncompromising truths that pushed them forward, that drove and directed their decisions to give their lives for a great cause.

In our own lives, it's no different. There are many things that we do in life that we don't necessarily believe in. These activities rarely have lasting value for us. Often they go unfinished or are done completely half-heartedly. But there are things in life that we will give our all to. Why? Because they are direct reflections of our deepest held values.

Early in my Real Estate career, I made a presentation for a large tenant representation assignment. I worked my butt off and found myself "needing" the large commission it would bring. I did not get the assignment. For two weeks, I had trouble sleeping. I just could not let it go. I needed perspective. If I value work more than family, or peace of mind, or health, I lose sight of the important things in life. In that moment, I made a decision that I would *never* "need" another deal. Sure, I'm pissed off when I do not get assignments, but I do not lose sleep. I do not "need" any deals.

Values are foundational

Often we can confuse our core values with the things we value. For instance, I value money, but money is not a value for me. Rather, I value freedom. Money is a tool that allows me to have freedom. I only value money for what it can do to help me achieve my core value of freedom. If I made money a value, I'd actually sacrifice my foundational value of freedom because I'd become a slave to money. Sure, I work hard and put in long hours, but I do it for the freedom it brings me, not the money.

Our values are the foundation upon which we build our lives. Earlier in this book I shared the story of John. He ran one of the hardest races in the world in opposition to the values handed him. His dad told him he was no good and that he'd never amount to anything. John could've accepted those values as the truth and foundation for his life. Rather, John discovered his own values.

One value John knew to be true, in opposition to the value his dad gave him, was that he did have worth and that he could be something great through hard work, in spite of challenges, adversity, or naysayers. John ran and finished the Marathon des Sables because he built his life on that value. Of course, he wanted to prove his old man wrong, but more important he wanted to prove something to himself.

For better or for worse, our values drive our actions in life. And what we achieve in this life is built upon the values we hold.

Know your values

This idea of values is a double-edged sword. Because our actions are driven by our values, it's vital that we know and understand what they are. Unfortunately, many people never put much thought into their values. They end up with inherited values from those who raised them and from the surrounding culture—some of them good and some of them bad.

Marshall McLuhan, the famed Canadian philosopher, said, "All media exists to invest our lives with artificial perceptions and arbitrary values." His point was that when passively received, our culture creates values for us that may not be true or even helpful, but they, though arbitrary, become our values by default. And those values then drive our actions.

This explains much of what goes wrong in our lives. For instance, those who value comfort often turn to addictive substances to numb the pain when they find that life is often not comfortable and instead requires sacrifice and hard work. Those who value what others' think of them make decisions to buy things they can't afford and possibly don't want, such as clothes, houses, cars, and more, all in an effort to gain acceptance. Those who value money will often sacrifice family, friends, and their ethics to attain it. The examples can go on and on.

In our culture, we're often overwhelmed with information and media seeking to create our values for us. In this environment, it's essential that we become proactive in discovering what is really true for us—what our values really are. And it's even more essential that we use those values as the basis for all we do, that we allow our values to drive our behavior, not the other way around.

To live a *Fantastic Life*, you must be value-driven.

Action items

1. List the values by which you operate your life. Be honest in listing them. Don't list what values you want to live by. Instead, list the values that you're actually living by.

2. Evaluate that list and determine if they are true values that are important to you, or if they are values that you've inherited but don't necessarily believe in.

3. Determine what you really value.

4. Modify your list accordingly, deleting the values that you don't believe in and replacing them with those that you do.

5. Begin living your life by your true values.

Some helpful questions to ask

1. What decisions did I make in the last week that have long-term consequences?

2. Why did I make those decisions? What values drove my actions?

3. What values do I have that are my own? What values do I have that I've inherited without thought?

4. What do I truly believe about life and how it should be lived? Am I living out those values in my life?

5. If not, why? How can I begin to live by my true set of values?

Rule #8
Play Where You Can Win

All throughout the 2000's, *American Idol* was a television ratings powerhouse, averaging twenty to thirty million viewers. The show format was simple. Tens of thousands of hopeful pop stars auditioned for a spot to compete to become the American Idol. The prize for the winner was a record contract and instant fame.

Whether you're a fan of the show or not, chances are you've seen some of the worst auditions floating around the web. And they are horrific. If you Google "worst *American Idol* auditions," you'll find some particularly funny ones.

I feel for the judges who have to sit through these auditions. Often you'll see them lose control and start cracking up. Sometimes you'll see the pained expressions on their faces as they're forced to sit and listen to some of the worst singing in America. And the feedback, while honest, is especially harsh.

Simon Cowell, the harshest judge of them all, for instance, once told a contestant, "Last year, I described someone as being the worst singer in America. I think you're possibly the worst singer in the world based on that performance, and I'm absolutely serious." But perhaps the best word of advice came from Randy Jackson, who told one hapless singer, "This is not your thing, dog. This is not your thing."

Randy is right. In life there are some things that are simply not our "thing." The horrible singers that try out for *American Idol* are a good reminder that, in order to live the *Fantastic Life*, it's important to play where you can win. Otherwise, you're in for a world of hurt and disappointment.

The problem with self-esteem

Today, self-esteem reigns supreme. I'm not sure how it happened, but our culture has moved from one that acknowledges realities to one that seems to think anything is possible. You can see examples of this everywhere. Today, even if you play on the worst Little League team in town, everyone gets a trophy. The message: everyone's a winner. You'll often hear parents encourage their kids, "It's not whether you win or lose, it's how you play the game." This is true, in a sense, but too often it seems we reward kids even for playing poorly.

It's really not the kids' fault. It's ours. When we encourage them to play in a game they can't win, of course we need to find ways to make sure their confidence isn't totally crushed. But the reality is that they probably shouldn't have been playing in the first place. There are probably other areas in life where they could excel. It takes some honesty and fortitude to acknowledge that. And it actually sets the kids up for a bigger win in life when you instill a dose of reality and allow them to achieve true self-esteem through excelling at something they're good at rather than rewarding mediocrity.

Unfortunately, this self-esteem mentality doesn't stop at childhood. I've had a number of people come through my rigorous training program at Lee & Associates who had an entitlement complex. They didn't have the skill set to be a great commercial leasing agent, but they felt that they deserved it. It was a hard dose of truth when I had to let them go. I knew they'd never actually win at the game of leasing. I'm sure they could win somewhere, but not there. In our cubicle, we try to always, "Speak the Unspoken Truth."

If we're honest with ourselves, we know that while we can *try* anything, we can't *do* everything. Sometimes this is a natural consequence of biology. A short, uncoordinated guy is never going to play professional basketball. A shy introvert is never going to be the CEO of a major corporation. Sometimes this is self-imposed. A lazy person isn't going to succeed in the world of business. Someone who can't keep his temper isn't going to have a happy marriage.

I'm not saying that self-esteem isn't important. It is. But self-esteem isn't worth much if it's derived from being told we can do anything, only to fail when reality sets in. The goal shouldn't be to force a win in an area where it's not possible; it should be to find the place where you can win. That's how you develop true self-esteem. You need to play where you can win.

See reality

Jack Welch, the former Chairman and CEO of General Electric, has a great saying, "Face reality as it is, not as it was or as you wish it to be." Jack's point is one that we'd all do well to take to heart.

A great example of living Jack's ethos of seeing reality as it is would be Nick Vujicic. Nick's story is truly heroic. Born without any legs or arms, Nick faced more adversity and obstacles in life than most of us can ever imagine.

As a child, Nick struggled to find his self-esteem. As you would guess, he faced his share of ridicule, teasing, and taunting from fellow classmates. He was often bullied, and he constantly questioned why he was so different from everyone else. By the age of eight, Nick battled depression and contemplated suicide. At age ten, he tried to drown himself in the bathtub, but stopped short out of love for his parents.

For years, Nick prayed that his legs and arms would grow out and that he'd live a normal life. Those prayers were never answered. A turning point for Nick was when he studied the lives of others who were disabled and was amazed at their accomplishments. He decided to face his life as it was, not as he wished it to be.

Despite his disability, Nick taught himself how to write with the two toes on his left foot and to type on a computer using his heels and toes. He even learned to throw tennis balls, play drum pedals, get a glass of water, comb his hair, brush his teeth, answer the phone, and shave—all without any arms and legs.

Today, Nick is a sought after motivational speaker who has authored a book and produced a number of DVDs to encourage young people. To date, he's spoken to over 3 million people in over twenty-four countries, has been interviewed by *20/20*, and is married and expecting his first child. Nick says, "We all have limitations. I'll never be an NBA star, but that's ok because I can inspire people to be the stars of their own lives." That is the spirit of a man who sees reality as it is, not as it was or how he wished it to be.

Just like Nick, we all have limitations. They may not be as severe as missing our arms or legs, but they are just as real and, in their own ways, just as debilitating if we don't acknowledge them and respond accordingly. The key to living the *Fantastic Life* is to know what your limitations are and to work out of your strengths.

Find your strength

It does you no good to simply dwell on your weaknesses and limitations. That is definitely a recipe for low self-esteem. Instead, it's important to discover what your strengths are. Where can you excel? What unique abilities do you bring to the table? Often what we're best at is discovered through failure. Try everything you want to do, but don't think for a moment that you'll succeed at everything. Rather, little by little, discover what you're really good at and keep pushing forward. That's the value that failure brings to the table.

As you begin to find your strengths, apply them in areas where you can win. If you're excellent at math and subpar at English, don't try to be a writer. Be the best mathematician you can be. Help run a company as a CFO. Or excel at computer programming. Those are the areas where you can win, and playing where you can win will lead to a *Fantastic Life* full of opportunities, where the sky really is the limit.

Become the strongest

Once you find your strength and where you can win, apply everything you have to being the best. Always be growing. Have a bathtub full of ambition. It's your ambition that will allow you to hone and grow your capabilities. It's this kind of focus and dedication that separates the best from the rest. Those who know what they're good at, where they can win, and who give it the 110 percent are the ones that succeed the most in life.

Action items

1. Examine the areas in your life where you're putting in the most effort.

2. Determine if you're working from your strengths in those areas or from your weaknesses.

3. Write down the things you want to do but haven't started yet.

4. Determine if those are areas of strength or weakness.

5. Remove yourself from areas where you can't win and position yourself to be in areas where you can.

Some helpful questions to ask

1. What am I good at?

2. What are my weaknesses? Be honest.

3. What areas of my life am I working out of my weaknesses? Why?

4. What areas of my life am I working out of my strengths?

5. How can I begin to remove myself from working out of my weaknesses and begin playing where I can win?

#3—*Steps to achievement*

Once you've defined your goal and set a target date, you need to break it up with measurable and achievable steps to get you to the finish line. In our losing weight example, it would look like this.

- Go to the gym on Mondays, Wednesdays, and Fridays with an outdoor activity on the weekends. Date: Start this Monday. You should put the workout dates on your calendar and track each one.

- Start a new diet eating nutrient-rich whole foods. Date: Today. Track your meals and calories daily.

- First 5 pounds lost. Date: End of month one.

- Cut television viewing by three hours per week. Date: Starting Monday.

- Next 5 pounds. Date: End of month two.

- Last 5 pounds. Date: End of month three.

#4—*List of obstacles*

There are many things that get in the way of us reaching our goals. Going back to our losing weight example, the list of obstacles could look like this:

- Getting up at five o'clock in the morning three days a week to go to the gym.

- The salty and sugary snacks in my kitchen.

- Peer pressure from friends who aren't dieting and exercising.

Rule #9
Set Goals

Each of us, whether we consciously know it or not, are ruled by our habits. Life is habits, and like life, we can have both good habits and bad habits. Some are obvious, like the habit of smoking. It's a bad habit that's bad for you. Others are not as obvious, such as body language habits that put those around you at unease.

In speaking of habits, the British writer and philosopher, Samuel Johnson said, "Habits are first cobwebs, then cables. The chains of habit are too weak to be felt until they are too strong to be broken." Essentially, what Johnson is saying is that most of us are ruled by our habits instead of ruling our habits. Most people don't set out to have bad habits, but instead they slowly develop them until it feels nearly impossible to break them.

But not all habits are sneaky like this. The good ones, especially, often take a focused and intentional person to develop them. For instance, developing the habit of good eating takes intentionally saying, "No," to a lot of the junk that is put in front of us. Developing the habit of being punctual takes the conscious decision to be so, time and time again.

It seems that most of our good habits take fighting against our natural gravitation towards bad habits. But understanding this is half the battle.

Since life is habits, it follows that it's important to form good ones. The most successful people I know are those who have good habits, such as a strong work ethic, getting up early, saying thank you, and being on time. They're not mind-blowing, but they're important. And perhaps the most important habit I've seen in successful people is the habit of goals.

What is a goal?

In the last few chapters, we've talked a lot about ways to accomplish goals. In this chapter I want to take a moment to talk about goals themselves.

A good working definition of a goal comes from author Napoleon Hill, "A goal is a dream with a deadline."

Different types of goals include our diet, exercise, professional life, family, friends, spiritual life, money, and more. We all have things we want to accomplish in these areas, but more often than not, our dreams go unfulfilled. Why? The most common reason is because we don't place a deadline on ourselves to accomplish them. Without a deadline, our dreams may never have the chance to become reality. This is because life is busy. If you're not planning for the future, in a concrete way, the cares of today will always take over the dreams of tomorrow.

When you set a goal by placing a deadline on your dream, you make it something that can be accomplished. But a deadline is not enough. You must break your goals down into components that can be achieved individually to make up the sum of your ultimate goal.

The four elements of a goal

In order to be best achieved, a goal must have four components.

#1—A goal must be specific

It does you no good to have a goal that is ethereal. In order to be achievable, a goal must be tangible. You must see, touch, and feel it. So, for instance, if you want to bulk up through weight training, it's not enough to say, "I want to build muscle." A better way is to have a picture of someone who you want to look like in regards to your muscle tone and to build to that.

#2—A goal must be measurable

In addition to the goal being specific, you must be able to measure it. You can't just say you want to lose weight; you need to say that you want to lose ten, fifteen, or twenty pounds. By doing this you create a baseline to work toward that can easily be measured each day.

#3—A goal must have a deadline

As discussed earlier, you need a deadline to achieve this goal. Going back to our example of losing weight, you need to say you want to lose fifteen pounds in three months. This will determine the steps you need to make in those three months to achieve your goal.

#4—A goal must be written

Finally, you need to write your goal down. It's easy to say something, and just as easy to push it to the side if it's not put down on paper. Writing your goals down makes them harder to ignore and easier to attain, especially when your goals are involved and take a number of steps to achieve. Just like you would make a plan for anything else important in your life, you need to make a written plan for your goals.

The anatomy of a goal

If you took anatomy in college, you know the complexity of the human body. If you're planning on being a doctor or biologist, understanding how each component of the body works together gives you insight into how to treat and study it.

The same is true for our goals. They seem deceptively simple on the surface, but just like our bodies, a goal is a complex organism that requires both a micro and macro understanding.

Dan Sullivan, founder of the Strategic Coach, illustrates successful steps to Goal Setting in his innovative knowledge product called The Strategy Circle[®1]. The Strategy Circle[®] breaks down Goal Setting into the following steps:

#1—Define the result

This involves understanding the specific and measurable result of accomplishing your goal. An example would be, "I'm going to fit into my old jeans by losing fifteen pounds." A result must have a number or a date attached to it.

#2—Target date

Along with the specific and measurable definition of the goal, you also have a deadline. "I'm going to fit into my old jeans by losing fifteen pounds in the next three months."

- Not seeing immediate results.

- Getting discouraged from slip-ups.

#5—*Strategy for each obstacle*

Next you need to create a strategy for overcoming each obstacle. As Dan says, "Obstacles are actually the raw materials for reaching your goals." By doing this, you will be in a position to win rather than be conquered by your obstacles when they come. It could look like this:

- Set two alarms, one in my room and one that forces me to get up to turn it off.

- Remove all junk food from the house and stock up on healthy options. Have a friend or spouse keep me accountable each time I go shopping.

- Have a speech ready for the times when peer pressure comes and ask friends to help you by not tempting you. Turn negative peer pressure into positive peer pressure.

- Don't measure success by where I want to be, but instead by where I've been. If I'm not losing weight as fast as I want, find encouragement in achieving my goals of working out and eating better. If I'm still not losing weight, figure out why and adjust my strategy, but don't take it as personal defeat.

- If I slip up, revisit my written goals and my tracked progress to re-center. Don't give up.

#6—Daily action

Meeting your goal takes daily action. Whether it's going to the gym, saying no to junk food, or reviewing your goals and progress, you should do something associated with your goal each day to make progress in little steps and keep it at the top of your mind.

#7—Weekly and monthly review

As we've already discussed in the points above, it's crucial that you review your progress and make adjustments as necessary. It takes tight management and personal discipline to accomplish a goal. It never happens on autopilot.

This process in action: training for the Tae Kwon Do World Championships

I practiced Tae Kwon Do for many years and have a number of black belts. In 2004, I had an once-in-a-lifetime opportunity to be a part of the U.S. Tae Kwon Do World Championship team. The team consisted of five *really* talented guys who had committed their life to the sport, and then there was me. I was just kind of good, but they brought me in thinking they could hide me as the sixth guy. What they didn't know was the process and discipline I would bring to the table.

I brought a schedule and showed up both mentally and physically during our daily training, forcing everyone to be better. We had a goal to win the championship, and I had the plan we needed.

Following is the schedule I produced.

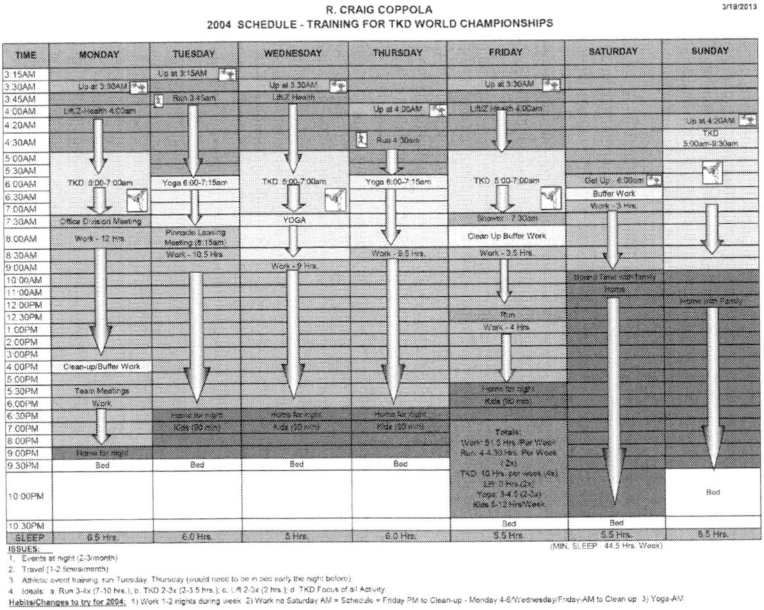

R. CRAIG COPPOLA
2004 SCHEDULE - TRAINING FOR TKD WORLD CHAMPIONSHIPS

3/19/2013

TIME	MONDAY	TUESDAY	WEDNESDAY	THURSDAY	FRIDAY	SATURDAY	SUNDAY
3:15AM		Up at 3:15AM					
3:30AM	Up at 3:30AM		Up at 3:30AM		Up at 3:30AM		
3:45AM		Run 3:45am	Lift/Z Health				
4:00AM	Lift/Z-Health 4:00am			Up at 4:00AM	Lift/Z Health 4:00am		
4:20AM							Up at 4:20AM
4:30AM				Run 4:30am			TKD 5:00am-9:30am
5:00AM							
5:30AM							
6:00AM	TKD 5:00-7:00am	Yoga 6:00-7:15am	TKD 5:00-7:00am	Yoga 6:00-7:15am	TKD 5:00-7:00am	Get Up - 6:00am	
6:30AM						Buffer Work	
7:00AM						Work - 3 Hrs.	
7:30AM	Office Division Meeting		YOGA		Shower - 7:30am		
8:00AM	Work - 12 Hrs	Pinnacle Leasing Meeting (8:15am)			Clean Up Buffer Work		
8:30AM		Work - 10.5 Hrs		Work - 8.5 Hrs.	Work - 3.5 Hrs.		
9:00AM			Work - 9 Hrs.				
10:00AM						Spend Time with family	
11:00AM						Home	
12:00PM							Home with Family
12:30PM					Run		
1:00PM					Work - 4 Hrs		
2:00PM							
3:00PM							
4:00PM	Clean-up/Buffer Work						
5:00PM							
5:30PM	Team Meetings				Home for night		
6:00PM	Work				Kids (90 min)		
6:30PM		Home for night	Home for night	Home for night			
7:00PM		Kids (90 min)	Kids (90 min)	Kids (90 min)	Totals: Work 51.5 Hrs /Per Week Run 4-4.30 Hrs. Per Week (2x) TKD 10 Hrs. per week (4x) Lift 3 Hrs (2x) Yoga 3-4.5 (2-3x) Kids 8-12 Hrs/Week		
8:00PM							
9:00PM	Home for night						
9:30PM	Bed	Bed	Bed	Bed			
10:00PM							Bed
10:30PM					Bed	Bed	
SLEEP	6.5 Hrs.	6.0 Hrs.	5 Hrs.	6.0 Hrs.	5.5 Hrs.	5.5 Hrs.	6.5 Hrs.

(MIN. SLEEP - 44.5 Hrs. Week)

ISSUES:
1. Events at night (2-3/month)
2. Travel (1-2 times/month)
3. Athletic event training, run Tuesday, Thursday (would need to be in bed early the night before).
4. Ideals: a. Run 3-4x (7-10 hrs.); b. TKD 2-3x (2-3.5 hrs.); c. Lift 2-3x (2 hrs.); d. TKD Focus of all Activity.

Habits/Changes to try for 2004: 1) Work 1-2 nights during week 2) Work no Saturday AM = Schedule = Friday PM to Clean-up - Monday 4-6/Wednesday/Friday-AM to Clean up 3) Yoga-AM

We defined the goal: to feel the medals around our necks. We set a date: to win in a year's time. The training schedule listed steps needed to train for the event in order to win. We defined the obstacles that needed to be worked around, mainly time, and how to fit the training around those constraints. The plan required daily action to accomplish.

It wasn't easy (you'll notice we didn't sleep much), but it was worth it. We won the championship that year. We accomplished our goal. They've never won it since. Two years later, when they lost in the first round, they called me and said, "You know why we lost? Because we didn't have you and your plan."

That's the power of setting goals in a way that sets you up to win.

Last word: get in

The only way to achieve your goals is to start today. Jump in with both feet. Don't be intimidated by this chapter; be emboldened. You can do it. Get in.

Action items

1. Determine your goals, defining them specifically.

2. Set target dates for your goals.

3. List out the steps needed to achieve your goals.

4. List the obstacles in the way and a strategy for each.

5. Take daily action on your plan and always review.

Some helpful questions to ask

1. If the idea of setting this comprehensive plan for goals intimidates me, why?

2. Have I achieved the goals I've set before? Why or why not?

3. What changes can I make in my life, now, to begin meeting my goals?

4. What are the obstacles holding me back? Why are they getting in the way and how can I overcome them?

5. How am I doing with my plan? Do I need to make adjustments?

[1] The Strategy Circle® is a registered trademark, protected by copyright, and an integral concept of Strategic Coach®, Inc. All rights reserved. Used with written permission. For more information on the Strategic Coach® Program or The Strategy Circle®, please visit www.strategiccoach.com.

Rule #10
Stay Out of The Gap™

Parkour is an emerging sport worldwide. If you go to YouTube and watch some of the Parkour videos posted, you'll be amazed. These are guys who leap from one building to another, sometimes landing on skinny beams and still retain their balance. They'll drop thirty feet or more and land on their feet without injury. Some of the advanced practitioners can run up and across walls. It's almost unbelievable some of the stuff that they can do.

When you see their feats, the first thing you'll probably think is, "Those guys are crazy." The second thing you'll think is, "How do they do that?"

As much as it's a sport, Parkour is also a philosophy of life. As Mark Toorock, one of the world's most renowned discipline of Parkour explained to *The New Yorker*, "A key factor in Parkour is gradualism. You can't find the highest thing to jump from in order to practice your rolls. You get down on the ground first and practice your rolls, and then maybe you find something three feet high to launch yourself from. When you can do something correctly a hundred times out of a hundred, you increase your task. Maybe. If you feel confident. People wonder how David Belle can leap between buildings and fall thirty feet. He started low and built up the difficulty."

Key to the Parkour philosophy is the idea of continual progress; progress that comes in steps that require being better than you were before. No one can start with the goal of jumping thirty feet and measure their success by whether they make the jump. Rather, they measure their success by how much better they did than before.

As Toorock says, "Everyone's different, but the philosophy of Parkour that drives me is that progression of ability, being better than I was the day before. There's a quote by Bruce Lee that's my motto: 'There are no limits. There are plateaus, but you must not stay there, you must go beyond them. A man must constantly exceed his level.' If you're not better than you were the day before, then what are you doing—what's the point?"

Lofty goals are important

A key part of life is continually moving forward and growing. If you're not doing that, you're not really living. The only things that don't grow are dead things. In our lives, one way to know we're moving forward and growing is by having goals that we're trying to reach. And, generally, the bigger the goal, the better.

The good news about our goals is that with focus and priorities, we can be successful. But you probably know many people who set lofty goals yet never achieve them. Most likely, you've experienced that yourself. The question is, why? What holds us back from attaining our goals?

The Gap

My friend and coach, Dan Sullivan, creator of the the Strategic Coach® Program, has helped me to understand why we don't achieve our goals. He says the biggest problem is being in The Gap™2.

Most people have an "ideal" of where they want to be. The ideal is like the horizon. It is not attainable. When you get to the horizon, it has moved further away.

The Gap™ is the space between where you are now and where you want to be. Unfortunately, most people measure success by that space. This is The Gap™ that Dan talks about.

The problem with living in The Gap™ is that we become discouraged because of the distance between our reality and our ideal. (Remember, the ideal is never attainable.)

The Negative Zone

The key to Dan's insight is that, for all individuals, happiness requires continual achievement in our personal and professional life. The problem is that most people live in a Negative Zone. They have a mindset that sets them up for failure by measuring their achievement by where they want to be rather than by where they've been. Rather than say, "Look at all the progress I've made," they say,

"Look at how far I have to go." This mindset creates a cycle of negativity and discouragement that makes it impossible for them to be happy.

As Dan says, those who live in The Gap, who are in the Negative Zone, grow unhappier with their achievements because they measure their progress by their ideals.

Those in the Negative Zone experience achievement as failure. They:

A. Visualize an "ideal" future that enables them to identify bigger and better goals.

B. Progress forward and achieve those goals, which can be in any experience of life.

C. Measure their very real achievements forward against their ideals and always experience feelings of failure, frustration, and disappointment.

Does that sound familiar to you? Don't be surprised if it does. Most people live their lives this way.

The Positive Zone

For Dan, the key to happiness is getting out of the Negative Zone and moving into the Positive Zone. Those in the Positive Zone have a single mental strategy and habit that makes it possible for them to get more and more positive energy and rewards from forward progress over their entire lifetimes.

Those who live in the Positive Zone measure their progress and achievement backward against their "start" points. Because they do this, they always have a growing sense of success and growth. When you're in the Positive Zone, you look at achievement as success.

Much like those in the Negative Zone, you still:

A. Visualize an "ideal" future that enables you to identify bigger and better goals.

B. Progress forward and achieve those goals, which can be in any area of life.

But unlike those in the Negative Zone, those in the Positive Zone measure the first two steps differently. They:

C. Measure every achievement, big or small, backward from where they were to where they are now.

This gives a continual sense of success and satisfaction.

Avoiding The Gap

Simply said, avoiding The Gap™ means *visualizing* forward, achieving bigger and better goals, and *measuring* backward to gain a sense of accomplishment. That's the key to happiness and success.

Going back to my example of Parkour, it's not hard to see how this is played out practically. Those who practice Parkour jump across very real gaps, often with a hundred feet below them, by staying out of The Gap™ mentally. Can you imagine if they measured their success by whether or not they could make the leap from one building to another? They'd fail—and probably kill themselves in the process.

Rather, those who practice Parkour train incrementally by starting small and making progressive steps towards their big goal. This means that they don't start with a goal to leap from building to building and feel like they've failed when they don't make it. Instead, they first master the ability to jump from a small wall to a small wall. They look at that as a success that moves them closer to their big goal. They jumped farther and better today than they did yesterday. Eventually, they reach their big, lofty goal, and then they're thinking higher and higher.

You might not be trying to leap across tall buildings, but there's a good chance you have some lofty goals you want to accomplish. If you want to succeed in those goals, take a cue from Parkour practitioners and from Dan Sullivan—stay out of The Gap™ and start measuring your success by where you were to where you are. If you do that, you can achieve more than you ever imagined.

Action items

1. Visualize your ideal future.

2. Set goals to achieve that ideal.

3. Celebrate each goal achieved.

4. Begin measuring your progress by looking backward.

5. Stay out of The Gap!

Some helpful questions to ask

1. What is my ideal life? Where do I want to be in one, five, ten years and beyond?

2. What are the steps I'll need to make to achieve my ideal?

3. If I'm honest, do I feel discouraged or encouraged when it comes to achieving my ideal? Am I happy or unhappy?

4. Am I measuring my success by where I want to be or by where I've been? Why?

5. Where have I been in the last day, week, month, and year? Where am I now? How far have I grown?

[2] The Gap™ is a trademark, protected by copyright and an integral concept of the Strategic Coach®, Inc. All rights reserved. Used with written permission. www.strategiccoach.com.

Rule #11
The Growth Paradigm

Last chapter we talked about the necessity of growth. In this chapter, I want to dig a little deeper into the concept of growth. In my experience, I think there are three ways in which we grow: slow and steady, the big hit, and bam—what I call the Growth Paradigm. Understanding the Growth Paradigm will help you to navigate life better and react appropriately to change.

Slow and steady growth

The last chapter focused on this type of growth. It's the slow, incremental steps you take day in and day out to be better than you were before. This is a measurable growth, using where you were as the baseline for seeing how far you have grown.

A good example of this type of growth would be training for a marathon. No one can start out ready to run a marathon, even if you're in good shape. Running over 26 miles is a grueling task that takes both physical and mental discipline and training. It's not something you take on lightly, but it's something that anyone can do if they put in the work.

It takes slow and steady growth to be in shape for a marathon. In my training, I established a 16 week program to be in shape for a race, because there are many factors involved in running a successful marathon: pacing, endurance, and stamina. My training involves a mixture of cross-training, easy short runs, tempo runs, long runs, pace runs, and rest. Here's an example schedule:

Mileage Chart

Week	Monday	Tuesday	Wednesday	Thursday	Friday	Saturday	Sunday
1	xtrain	easy	tempo	easy	rest	pace	long
	1 hour	3	5	3	0	5	10
2	xtrain	easy	tempo	easy	rest	easy	long
	1 hour	3	6	3	0	6	8
3	xtrain	easy	tempo	easy	rest	pace	long
	1 hour	3	6	3	0	6	13
4	xtrain	easy	tempo	easy	rest	pace	long
	1 hour	3	7	3	[illegible]	[illegible]	14
5	xtrain	easy	tempo	[illegible]	[illegible]	[illegible]	pace
	1 hour	3	7	[illegible]	[illegible]	[illegible]	15k
6	[illegible]	[illegible]	[illegible]	[illegible]	[illegible]	[illegible]	long
	[illegible]	[illegible]	[illegible]	[illegible]	[illegible]	[illegible]	16
7	[illegible]	[illegible]	[illegible]	[illegible]	[illegible]	[illegible]	long
	[illegible]	[illegible]	[illegible]	[illegible]	[illegible]	[illegible]	12
8	[illegible]	[illegible]	[illegible]	[illegible]	[illegible]	[illegible]	long
	[illegible]	[illegible]	[illegible]	[illegible]	[illegible]	[illegible]	19
9	[illegible]	[illegible]	[illegible]	[illegible]	[illegible]	[illegible]	long
	[illegible]	[illegible]	[illegible]	[illegible]	[illegible]	[illegible]	20
10	[illegible]	[illegible]	[illegible]	[illegible]	rest	easy	pace
	[illegible]	[illegible]	[illegible]	5	0	6	20-25k
11	[illegible]	[illegible]	[illegible]	easy	rest	pace	long
	1 hour	5	10	5	0	10	20
12	xtrain	easy	tempo	easy	rest	easy	long
	1 hour	5	6	5	0	6	12
13	xtrain	easy	tempo	easy	rest	pace	long
	1 hour	5	10	5	0	10	20
14	xtrain	easy	tempo	easy	rest	easy	race
	1 hour	5	8	5	0	4	10-k
15	xtrain	easy	tempo	easy	rest	easy	long
	45 min.	4	6	4	0	4	8
16	xtrain	easy	tempo	easy	rest	easy	MARATHON
	30 min.	3	4	0	0	1-3	

This schedule is appropriate for both first-time and experienced marathoners with a base of at least 20-25 miles per week.

As you can see from this chart, there are very few times in my training where I actually run the length of a marathon. Instead, I focus on training for various aspects of running that I will face during the race. Mondays are for strength training. Tuesdays are for cardio upkeep. Wednesdays are for tempo training, mixing in faster and slower paces. Thursdays are another easy run to keep my body in running shape. Friday is a rest day to allow the body to heal. Saturday is a pace run, going longer and farther distances at an optimal speed (until a few weeks before the race and then I take it easy). And Sunday is the day for longer runs to develop the mental disciple to finish a race. It's only when I do the actual race that all this training comes together into one. If I've trained well, I'll run a good race.

Each day, I record my times and accomplishments for a particular training module. I can then look back and see how much progress I've made. I want to be doing better today than I did yesterday. That is slow and steady growth that, if done right, will lead to the accomplishment of my big goal: running a great marathon.

This type of discipline is applicable to anything we want to do in life. With big goals, you break down the task into measurable units that can be accomplished over time with steady growth. It's not an overnight solution, but it works. This is how we accomplish most things we want out of life.

Big hit growth

While slow and steady growth is the foundational growth for our lives, there are those rare moments in life when we have a chance to shoot for the stars. I call this big hit growth.

In business, this is the idea of *the* big deal. The one, life-changing deal, that if it hits, you're golden. It's the kind of growth that, if it happens, forces you to change a lot of things. These types of growth opportunities don't come around often, but when they do, you need to be ready for them.

For instance, in addition to my business, Lee & Associates—which is a business that I've grown slowly and steadily and that provides great steady returns—I also do angel investing for start-ups. In angel investing, I'll provide a sum of capital for a business or product that I think *might* take off. If the business or product fails, I lose everything. If it takes off, it's a huge return. Over the years, I've done about twenty of these types of deals—and fourteen of them have failed! But two have taken off, and four others are still in the game. Those investments could be huge home runs, real game-changers. Or they might not. But they're big hits I'm willing to bet on.

In my opinion, most of life should be planned and lived on a slow and steady pace, but everyone should be looking for 10 to 20 big-hit opportunities to get involved in over their lifetime. The risk is high, but the reward could be worth it.

Unfortunately, a lot of people live their life trying to get a big hit instead of being slow and steady. The result is a lot of failed deals and a lot of heartache. The better way is to have a good foundation of growth that allows you to go for a big hit without losing everything.

Bam growth

The final type of growth is bam growth. It's unexpected, hits you like a ton of bricks, and is often painful. But it's the type of growth that gives you a different perspective on life. It's life throwing you a curve ball, and it changes you in ways you couldn't even imagine.

Perhaps a story would be the best way to illustrate this type of growth.

Everybody who knew Daisy adored her. A vibrant, quirky five-year old girl who loved costumes, play dates with friends, and constant discovery, Daisy was a special kind of child.

In September of 2009, during her first month of kindergarten, Daisy fell while on the playground and couldn't get up. Rushed to the hospital, upon examination, it was discovered that Daisy had cancer.

As Daisy's parents recount on their blog, "Daisy underwent a lengthy surgery to remove her Wilms' tumor, which was the size of a Nerf football and took up most of her abdominal cavity. Following the surgery, she was left with only one kidney. She underwent difficult treatments of chemotherapy and radiation. She lost her beautiful, golden hair, her eyelashes and eyebrows, and much of her energy. For many months, she was unable to leave the hospital or her house."

After long and painful treatments, Daisy was finally cancer free. The family celebrated and rejoiced only to find out a short time later that the cancer had returned. After more difficult treatments, Daisy was cancer free again, but the hard road wasn't over for the family.

After her second battle with cancer, the family counted each day as a gift. Daisy began taking horseback riding lessons, dancing jazz and ballet, and enjoying friends without fear of germs. She played with her brother, Isaiah, fell asleep with her dog, Sugar, kissed her mom and dad and sang songs to her Savior. For twelve months, she lived, laughed, and played like any normal seven-year-old, and her beautiful golden hair grew and curled to her shoulders. Hope was restored and all things seemed new. Until the day that Daisy went in for a routine scan, and the dreaded words were spoken for a third time: "Daisy has cancer yet again."

Little Daisy fought this third round of cancer hard, but on February 16, 2013, she finally lost her battle. Her mother shared the moving last moments they spent with their little girl:

"Our darling girl gave us kisses at midnight, with lips dry from thirst and hot with fever. Tiny and sweet, the words 'that's awesome' came from her tired body after letting us know she was having good dreams. She is safely home…Finally well. I have refrained from giving details of her suffering over the last few weeks, as it was immense. Out of respect for her dignity and loveliness we have been keeping these painful moments sacred…. On her last night on earth, she requested we watch 'The Hobbit' (70's version) and dress like hobbits. If ever there was a girl confident in her own skin, it was her. Among her favorite ensembles are animal ears of all kinds, astronaut, flightsuit, monster, pirate, dinosaur, Indian, mermaid, bear, cowgirl, fireman and explorer."

And then, they shared something of value for all parents that this experience had taught them:

"My final request to all who read this blog: love. Love your babies, your husbands, mothers, sisters. Love each day like it's your last. All you mamas out there, you have been entrusted with the precious gift of a human life who depends on you. Enjoy your gift. Breathe in the scent of your child's hair, breath. Let them cook with you and make a mess of the kitchen. Play hide and seek with them, build sand castles with them, take them on picnics, read to them! Listen to them, value and respect them, never shame them. Your words they will carry with them their whole life and you have the power to give them wings or stunt their growth. Motherhood can be tough but it's worth it. It can be exhausting, boring, tedious, but never for long. You blink and they're grown. It has been my honor and privilege to love Daisy these last 8 years. I'm thankful for every minute; the joyful and the terrible alike."

Bam growth is few and far between, but we'll all face it. And when it comes, it's big. It's not always tragic like Daisy's story, but it is always life-changing.

Be prepared for all three types of growth

In your life, I guarantee you'll face all three types of growth in the Growth Paradigm. The key to a *Fantastic Life* is to spend the majority of your time on the slow and steady, taking the big hit opportunities as they come, and being prepared to learn from the bam moments in life.

Action items

1. Determine if you're living your life on the slow and steady or if you're putting all your eggs in the big hit basket.

2. Think through how you can spend the majority of your life growing slow and steady and make an action plan.

3. Examine what big hit opportunities are in front of you and go after the ones you want the most.

4. Reflect on those bam growth moments of your life so far and draw out the lessons you've learned through those periods of growth.

5. Start recognizing what type of growth you're experiencing and prepare for all three types.

Some helpful questions to ask

1. What are the areas in my life where I should be experiencing slow and steady growth every day?

2. What big hit opportunities have I had up to this point? Why did they succeed or fail?

3. What big hit opportunities are in front of me? Do I want to pursue them? If so, how?

4. What bam moments have I had in life? What lessons can I draw from those?

5. How can I best prepare for the bam moments that will come down the road?

Rule #12
Get a Win

There's nothing better than the feeling after a run. As with anything hard, it's never easy to get going when you know you have a few miles ahead of you. I've been running for over twenty-five years and participated in more than eighty marathons. To accomplish this takes a lot of training. I get up at three thirty almost every morning to run at four o'clock. And you know what? It never gets easier. It's hard *every* morning. You'd think after all this time that it would be easier, but it's not.

Whether staring at a blank page when you're writing, or facing down a big to-do that's just waiting to be checked off, or running a few miles early each morning, sometimes the big tasks ahead of us seem almost impossible to start, let alone complete. But we all know how great the feeling is when we finally accomplish what we've set out to do, put in the miles, write that chapter, or check off that to-do.

Unfortunately, a lot of people take themselves out of the game before they even start because they're so overwhelmed by what has to be done to get to the finish line.

So, the question is, what can you do to accomplish your big goals? Part of the answer is, "Get a win."

Get a win

Get a win is a simple concept. It starts with what we talked about in Rule #10, staying out of The Gap. When we fail to accomplish our goals, it's usually because we're looking forward instead of backward. We see the finish line, but it's just too far out there for us to gather the gumption needed to move forward. So, we check out. We make excuses. We give up.

Getting a win allows us to go to bed at the end of the day and feel satisfied because we've accomplished something. It's a feeling of satisfaction that comes from knowing you didn't reach your full goal, but you did move towards it—instead of backwards or nowhere at all.

Getting a win starts with getting in a position to win

Getting a win starts with a change in mindset also called putting you in a position to win. Let me show you what I mean.

Recently, I went for a big hike, and I found it to be a lot harder than usual. I was huffing and puffing a little too much. The reason? I've packed on a few more pounds than I should.

So, I came home from this hike with a big goal in mind: lose some weight. Maybe you've tried to lose weight before. If so, you know that it's much easier said than done. When it comes to shedding pounds, it seems like there are a million little things each day that can put you in a position to lose. The key to sustained weight loss is to put yourself in a position to win.

For me, this meant eliminating temptations. A big way I put on weight is by eating too many carbs. When I came home, my wife had a bunch of cereal in the cupboards. I know my weaknesses, and honestly, a good bowl of cereal is one of them. So, I had to put myself in a position to win. This meant not hanging around the kitchen, where we would normally congregate. Instead, I spent more time on the trail and made sure to eat healthy. At times when I'd normally wander into the kitchen to snack, I mentally made a goal to not go into the kitchen and instead do something healthy. It wasn't a life-altering goal, but it was one that I could accomplish. I knew I could get a win.

The same thing is true for you. You might not be trying to lose weight, but whatever you're doing, I'm sure there are many small ways that you can put yourself in a position to win. Instead of focusing on your ultimate goal, focus on what you can accomplish right now.

Getting a position to win = small goals

Putting yourself in a position to win really means creating small goals that you can easily accomplish and with which you can make measurable progress. For me that meant going to bed at night and asking a simple question, "Did I eat any carbs today?" If the answer was, "No," then I got a win. It was easy to accomplish and helped me move forward towards my big goal of losing weight.

A good example of setting small, measurable, and accomplishable goals is a fellow runner friend of mine. He told me that each morning he has one goal, to get up and put his shoes on. That's all. It's not to run ten miles…or even one mile! It's simply to strap on a pair of sneakers.

"That's all I have to do," he says. "And if I decide at that point to just go out and make a pot of coffee with my running shoes on, I've done my goal. But what happens is that since I have my running shoes on, I decide I might as well go for a walk. And once I'm walking, I decide I might as well do my run. But it all starts with putting my shoes on in the morning. That's my goal."

Getting a win leads to more wins

My friend's story illustrates another important truth about getting a win: one win usually leads to another win. Putting on shoes leads to going for a walk. Going for a walk leads to going for a run. Going for a run leads to going for lots of runs. And going for lots of runs leads to being ready for a race.

Starting with the goal to be race ready is the opposite of getting a win. It usually leads to quitting. But almost everyone can put on a pair of shoes, or at least they should be able to!

Whatever you're trying to accomplish in life, it starts with getting a win. Because there's nothing better than hitting the sack at night knowing that you accomplished something, even if it wasn't life altering. As you keep getting little wins, before you know it, you'll have accomplished more than you imagined you could. And that's something to celebrate.

Action items

1. Write down one big goal that you're trying to accomplish now.

2. Make an assessment of how you're doing with that goal. Be honest.

3. Determine one thing that is small and accomplishable within that big goal that you can do today.

4. Get a win, today.

5. Determine another win you can get tomorrow and do it all over again.

Some helpful questions to ask

1. What big goals have I been putting off because they seem too big and overwhelming to start?

2. Which of these goals is the most important to me right now? Which of them can wait a little while longer?

3. What are some small steps I can do within my big goal in order to get a win each day?

4. As you get your wins, reflect each night on them. How does it feel to accomplish these small wins?

5. As you move along in the process, how are all your small wins adding up to your big win? Are you farther along than you were before you started? How do you feel?

Rule #13
The 2% Rule

Game five of the 1997 NBA Finals featured one of the most courageous performances in NBA history. With the series tied 2-2, the Chicago Bulls, led by Michael Jordan in his prime, came into Salt Lake City to play a pivotal game against the Jazz, led by league MVP Karl Malone, that would put one team on the inside track to the title.

Coming into the game, the Bulls felt confident. But that confidence was shattered when Jordan came down with severe flu-like symptoms the night before, which didn't go away come game time. By tip off, there was a very real concern that Jordan would be a non-factor in the game.

Steve Aschburner, writing for NBA.com, wrote about that night, "What I recall from my vantage point in the auxiliary media seating—at the top of the Delta Center's lower bowl—was that Jordan appeared loose, jangly, weak. His whole demeanor seemed a little fuzzy around the edges, his cuts not sharp and, even from that distance, a vacant sort of expression on his face. Only in close-ups, though, and mostly in replays could I see how glazed over his eyes were and how profusely he was sweating. Think Patrick Ewing. In a steam bath. After a 5K run. About to audition for 'Dancing With The Stars'—that's how badly it was pouring off Jordan."

After the first quarter, it seemed that Chicago's fears would come true. Jordan was a non-issue, struggling to make even simple shots, and the Jazz went up by sixteen points. But then, something clicked for Jordan. He scored seventeen points in the second quarter, lifting his team to within a few points at the half.

In the third quarter, however, fatigue and sickness once again got the best of Jordan. The game seemed to be slipping away. But again, Jordan was able to dig deep within himself in the fourth quarter, leading his team on a 10-0 run after being down 77-69.

"In the third quarter, I felt like I couldn't catch my wind and get my energy level up," Jordan said in a later interview, "I don't know how I got through the fourth quarter. I was just trying to gut myself through it."

What followed was NBA history in the making. Though exhausted and sick to his stomach, and dealing with intense headaches made only worse by the Utah altitude, Jordan led his team to victory, putting a dagger in the Jazz's heart with a three pointer to take the lead with only a few seconds left. By the game's end, Jordan had scored thirty-eight points, nabbed seven rebounds, dished five assists, and made three steals. The Bulls went on to win the NBA championship.

"I didn't want to give up," Jordan said. "No matter how sick I was, no matter how tired I was, no matter how low on energy I was. I felt an obligation to my teammates and the city of Chicago to go out and give that extra effort."

The 2% rule

A lot of people would be tempted to say that Jordan gave 100 percent that night in Utah. But if you stop and think for a moment, didn't he give much more than that?

A lot of motivational speakers are fond of saying, "Give 100 percent." It's a nice sentiment in theory, but in practice, giving 100 percent is actually limiting. Chances are, when you're told to give 100 percent, you equate that with giving your all. But there is another way of looking at it.

The problem with the phrase "Give 100 percent" is that it doesn't quantify what you're measuring. If it means giving your maximum effort, then you're setting yourself up to fail. Even the best athletes in the world can't sprint at peak capacity for more than a couple minutes. The most talented business people can't work 24/7, 365 days a year. There comes a time when you have to slow down and rest.

Another way of looking at 100 percent is to think of it as the maximum effort you can *consistently* maintain. When you look at it this way, it's clear that you can both underachieve *and* overachieve at points in your life.

Understanding "giving a 100 percent" this way makes it easy to understand why someone like Jordan can shock the sports world by digging deep inside himself to give "that extra effort," even when seriously ill. On that night in 1997, Jordan didn't give 100 percent; he gave much more. But how did he do that in the face of circumstances that would cause most people to tap out? The answer is found in The 2% Rule.

Simply put, The 2% Rule is forming the daily habit of doing just that much more than everyone else. Jordan didn't magically find a way to give more than a 100 percent to pull his team through. It was the culmination of a lifetime of doing more than he could for short periods of time, over a lifetime. This discipline allowed him to really dig deep when needed to go above and beyond.

Do 2% more than everyone else

Everyday, I ask my kids, "Did you give 2% more?" It doesn't matter what they were doing. What does matter is that they gave a little more than they thought they could. If they're doing homework, did they read through to double check their answers one more time? If they're training for a race, did they sprint the last 100 yards after running a couple miles?

Most successful people will stop at what is required. They'll finish their homework. They'll meet their sales quota. They'll put in the miles. But what separates champions from those who are simply successful is the habit of doing that little bit extra to push themselves beyond the norm.

Each day, you should ask yourself, "Did I do 2% more?"

Do 2% more every day

The thing about The 2% Rule is that it's a daily habit in all you do. You can't expect to really shine when the pressure is on if you haven't formed the consistent practice of doing more each day. This means that each day, you build on what you did yesterday. You're constantly creating a new baseline for what 100 percent looks like—and then going a little bit above and beyond. If you sprinted the last 100 yards yesterday, then maybe you do it uphill today. If you had ten sales calls yesterday, maybe you do twelve today. Did you give 2% more to a relationship? It doesn't matter where you apply the rule. What's most important is that you apply it consistently, every day.

The 2% Rule = exponential growth

The great thing about The 2% Rule is that it's exponential. Over time, as you look back on your progress, you can see how giving 2% each day grows exponentially to make a huge difference over time. This is how players like Jordan become great. It's how runners constantly beat their personal best. It's how top sales people consistently beat everyone else on the team. It is how marriages stay together. The growth pattern looks like this.

A GOAL is:

1)   A Dream with a Deadline.

2)   Four Elements of a Goal:

a) Specific
b) Measurable
c) Deadline
d) Written

3)   2% Rule ⟶

By doing 2% more, each and every day, you'll soon find that, come game time, whatever that means for you, you'll be heads and shoulders above your competition. It's little, achievable steps that add up big time at the end of the day.

Action items

1. Take stock of the effort you're putting into the most important things in your life.

2. Identify where you're giving your consistent best but not giving an extra 2% each day.

3. Establish a plan for how you can give that extra 2% each day.

4. Write down your goal each day and make sure to achieve it.

5. For motivation, look back after longer periods of time to see how far you've grown.

Some helpful questions to ask

1. Am I consistently giving my best, then 2% more, to the most important things in my life? Why or why not?

2. What are ways I can give my best, plus give that little bit extra each day?

3. When have I gone above and beyond? What did that look like, and how did I accomplish it? How did it feel?

4. What's something I can do today that is an extra 2%?

5. How can I keep myself accountable to give an extra 2% each day?

Rule #14
There are Two Kinds of Pain

On a gray 1992 day in Barcelona, British Olympic athlete, Derek Redmond, was preparing to run his semi-final 400-meter dash. There was a lot of hype surrounding the race and many were predicting that Derek had a shot at winning a medal. In the first round of the event, Derek had run his quickest race in years, and he was feeling good going into the semis.

As the gun went off, it seemed the hype was well founded. Derek was the quickest out of the blocks and was in a position to take the inner lane and command of the race. Then tragedy struck.

"On the day everything went smooth. I got a really good start, which was unusual for me. I think I was the first to react to the pistol. My normal tactics were to get round the first bend and then put the burners on for 30m, accelerate hard. But by the time I'd got upright I was almost round the bend, much further than usual, and I decided not to bother, to save my energy in case I had to fight for the line. About three strides later I felt a pop," Derek told *The Guardian* in a November 2011 interview. Derek's hamstring was torn and he hit the ground in pain.

After years and years of preparation and hard work, Derek's dream of winning an Olympic medal was shattered. It was a particularly painful moment for Derek because it was the latest in a series of heartbreaking injuries. He'd missed the 1986 Commonwealth Games with a hamstring injury and had to withdraw from the 1988 Seoul Olympics because he couldn't recover in time from tendinitis. He'd come close to giving up the sport all together but had worked hard to be ready for the 1992 games.

Everyone thought that Derek's race was done, but then the unthinkable happened. He got up and began limping along in an attempt to finish the race. The pain was excruciating, and you could see the struggle in his face to hold himself together.

"I got up quicker than I got out of the blocks," Derek told *The Guardian*. "I said to myself: 'There's no way I'm going to be stretchered out of these Olympics.'"

Derek's father, Jim, was in the stands. He'd been by his son's side since he first began training, cheering him on for years. Without a thought, Jim forced his way down the track to his weeping son, put his arms around his shoulder—pushing away officials who were trying to stop him—and helped carry his son all the way to the finish line, with Derek's face buried in his arms.

The crowd gave Derek a standing ovation as he crossed the line.

In a post-race interview, Derek's dad told the world, "But whatever happens, he had to finish, and I was there to help him finish. I intended to go over the line with him. We started his career together, and I think we should finish it together."

Pain is inevitable

In this life, pain is inevitable. The question is what kind of pain do you want? The way we view pain fundamentally shapes the way in which we live life.

Pain is necessary to grow. If you have kids, you know about growing pains, those annoying cramps that cause tears in the little ones as their bones and muscles stretch. It's pain that teaches us never to touch the hot stove again. It's pain that lets us know that we put in a solid workout. It's relational pain that makes healthy relationships so much more appreciated.

In pursuing a *Fantastic Life*, there are two types of pain that you will inevitably face: the pain of discipline or the pain of regret. You have the choice to face the one you want, but the reality is that they are unavoidable.

The pain of discipline

The pain of discipline is the pain that comes from having goals and dreams and putting in the work and commitment necessary to attain them. It's the pain of quitting your job to start a company, the pain of getting up at four o'clock in the morning to train for that marathon, the pain of late nights rocking your baby back to sleep, the pain of saying no to a new car and instead, investing your money. This pain comes in a lot of forms, but it's always a sacrificial pain.

The pain of discipline results in success purchased not at any one time, but on the installment plan. Each time we choose the pain of discipline, we move away from the pain of regret and move closer towards our goals. It's not a one-time decision but rather a daily decision. This pain is hard, and often it's felt immediately. But it also passes as we gain each little victory, transforming into a sense of accomplishment.

If, however, you choose to pass on the pain of discipline, you *automatically* choose the pain of regret.

The pain of regret

The pain of regret comes from not achieving our goals and dreams because we chose to pass on the pain of discipline it would take to get there. It's the pain that comes from not living up to our potential. It's *not* the pain that comes from failure, which is part of the learning process of living disciplined lives. Rather it comes from the failure to do what we know we could have and should have done to be where we wanted in life.

While we immediately feel the pain of discipline, the dangerous thing about the pain of regret is that we don't usually feel it until later. You feel it either hours, days, months, or even years later, when you look back and realize what you've squandered and the opportunities you've let pass by, in taking the road of comfort over the road of hard work.

The pain of regret doesn't go away. It sticks with you, right in your gut. And it hurts much worse than the pain of discipline.

Which pain will you choose?

When Derek Redmond hit the racetrack, his hamstring torn and unusable, he faced these two choices: the pain of discipline or the pain of regret. Would he stay down and always regret that he never finished the race? Or would he get up, and through extreme pain, finish the race injured? He chose the pain of discipline and finished the race with the help of his father. In the process, Derek became an inspiration for millions. A fellow competitor that he'd never met wrote to him after the race, saying, "Long after the names of the medalists have faded from our minds, you will be remembered for having finished, for having tried so hard, for having a father to demonstrate the strength of his love for his son. I thank you, and I will always remember your race and I will always remember you—the purest, most courageous example of grit and determination I have seen."

You probably won't ever face down the pain of your Olympic dreams being just over 100 meters away only to be derailed by a debilitating injury, but you do face the same choice as Derek every day in pursuit of your goals and dreams. The question is, will you choose the pain of regret or the pain of discipline? Your decision determines how far you can go.

Action items

1. Make a list of the goals and dreams that you have.

2. Make another list of the sacrifices it will take to attain them.

3. Take stock on whether you're choosing to make those sacrifices or are passing them up.

4. Ask if you're honestly choosing the pain of discipline or the pain of regret.

5. Begin choosing the pain of discipline.

Some helpful questions to ask

1. What do I want to accomplish in life?

2. What sacrifices will it take to do the things I want to do?

3. Where in the last week have I chosen the pain of regret rather than the pain of discipline? Why?

4. What can I begin doing right now to choose the pain of discipline over the pain of regret?

5. Who might I need to help me in my journey to finish my race?

Rule #15
Take the Decision Out of the Moment

A friend of mine's son started Little League this year. He describes watching the kids play as "the coaches trying to herd ants." Because the kids are just learning the rules of the game, they're never quite sure what to do when the ball is in play. When there's a hit, half of them go running after it, leaving their positions. If one of them fields the ball, he has to look around and think about where he's supposed to throw it. And when one of the kids gets a hit, it's not uncommon to hear all the coaches and parents in the stands yelling, "Run!"

Compare that level of play to that of professionals. A professional baseball game is a thing of art. Consider the speed of the game and the stakes on the line. Yet, professionals are able to perform almost without thought during the heat of the game. From snagging a fast line drive at third to turning a seemingly impossible double play, the speed at which a professional ball player reacts and performs necessitates instinctual play. There is no decision in the moment. They already know what to do.

In baseball, and in life, no one starts out ready to play on instinct. It takes years of preparation, study, and practice to get to the point where you instinctively know what you're supposed to do in the middle of fast-paced play. In fact, the average professional baseball player starts between the ages of five and seven, playing ball at every level. That's about fifteen to twenty years of instruction, practice, and preparation. And of course, they never stop practicing, even at the Big League level. Every aspect of the game is practiced over and over again with one goal: to perform without thinking come game time.

Life is a little like baseball

While most people won't play professional baseball, there's a lot to be learned from the sport when it comes to life. Like baseball, life has its slower moments and then, *wham*, the ball is in play and everything is moving fast. And just like in baseball, if we're not prepared, we'll look a lot like the kids in Little League, making a lot of mistakes while those who have prepared act on instinct, seeming to know what to do without thinking.

One of the keys to the *Fantastic Life* is to understand the importance of preparing so that you can take the decision out of the moment.

Living a big picture life

Tom Shrader runs a great program here in Arizona called "Priority Living." As part of the program, Tom shares that successful people live in light of the big picture. Living a big picture life is a combination of planning and action that allows us to have a filter for reacting to life, and when the heat comes, taking the decision out of the moment. The following are the components of a big picture life:

Mission

We all should have a grand purpose for why we exist. For some it's God, family, being generous, or being successful in business. Whatever your mission is in life, you often prioritize everything you do around it. It's important to understand that a mission is in fact a journey. It's never fulfilled. Otherwise we wouldn't have a reason to exist! Think of it like the horizon. You can keep walking towards it, but you never catch it.

Vision

Vision is the process of having a clear mental picture for your future in light of your mission. If mission is the horizon, vision is a point on the horizon that you work towards. You can reach that point, but there's always another point to go after.

Values

Our values are the uncompromising truths that drive and direct our behavior as we pursue our mission and live out our vision. If we sacrifice our values, we compromise our mission and sidetrack our vision. For instance, if family is your mission and being a good husband is your mission, a value you'll have is fidelity. If part of your vision is to be sober, having a drink detracts from your mission.

Goals

Goals, like we discussed previously, are dreams with a deadline. They're measurable objectives that help us achieve our mission and vision. Goals are individual components for living out our mission and vision.

Strategies

Strategies are a specific approach to achieve our goals. Going back to our baseball analogy from the beginning of this chapter, this is the game plan—the little things that you plan to practice to be game-day ready.

Tactics

Tactics are the implementation of your strategies. It's taking the practice plan and putting it into action, doing everything you need to be ready when the time comes.

Instinct begins with intention

Another way to think of a big picture life is to say you're living an intentional life. When you know your mission and vision, understand your values, set your goals, and execute your strategies through tactics, you build habits that form everything you do—and if you do it enough—you build instincts.

So going back to our family man, if your life is built around being a great husband and having a healthy family—and you've lived that with all your heart each and every day—when work starts taking over and you find yourself working nights and weekends, it's time to reset. Those who aren't prepared for such a temptation would have a much harder time saying no.

Or, if you're all about being a great businessperson with a foundation of rock-steady integrity, and an unethical deal opportunity came about, you'd be ready in the heat of that moment to pass. Knowing who you are, what you stand for, and where you're going allows you to take the decision out of the moment.

Far too often, we let life play us when we should be playing life. By living with intention, we're able to perform at peak performance when it comes to the game time of our life. Start living intentionally today and take the decision out of the moment.

Action items

1. Take stock of your life and determine if you're prepared to take the decision out of the moment.

2. Determine your mission in life and your vision for that mission.

3. List your values and remind yourself of them every day.

4. Set goals, like we talked about previously.

5. Each day, practice your *Fantastic Life* by having strategies and implementing tactics.

Some helpful questions to ask

1. Why do I exist? What drives everything I do? What's my mission?

2. How do I see my life in the next year? Where do I want to be in five years? Ten years?

3. What are my core values that I refuse to compromise on? How am I doing on holding up those values?

4. Am I living out my mission, vision, and values daily through strategies and tactics? How can I do this even better?

5. When my game-day comes, whatever that is for me, am I ready to act instinctively due to my preparation? Or do I need to work harder at being prepared? How?

Rule #16
Don't Waste Time

Everyone, at some point, procrastinates. Look up "overcoming procrastination" on Google and you'll find over 1,500,000 hits. According to *Psychology Today*, 20 percent of people chronically procrastinate. The great thinker Samuel Johnson described procrastination as "one of the general weaknesses" that "prevail to a greater or less degree in every mind."

Today, with so many distractions at our fingertips, the problem of procrastination only seems to be getting worse. According to business professor Piers Steel in an article in *The New Yorker* entitled, "What We Can Learn From Procrastination," the percentage of people who admitted to difficulties with procrastination quadrupled between 1978 and 2002. Each day we're tempted with dozens of opportunities to check out by surfing the web, fooling around on social media sites, watching unhealthy amounts of television, and more. We can access these things anywhere and any time through our computers and phones, creating constant temptation in our lives.

In fact, recent studies have shown that we spend over three hours a day interacting online through social media and surfing the web. That's a lot of wasted hours—and it doesn't even take into account television and other time-wasters. There's no doubt, time-wasting is an American epidemic.

Procrastination is bad for you

Yet, we all know how damaging procrastination can be for us. In the same *The New Yorker* article quoted earlier, author James Surowiecki points out that:

Each year, Americans waste hundreds of millions of dollars because they don't file their taxes on time. The Harvard economist David Laibson has shown that American workers have forgone huge amounts of money in matching 401(k) contributions because they never got around to signing up for a retirement plan. Seventy percent of patients suffering from glaucoma risk blindness because they don't use their eye drops regularly.

On a psychological level, procrastination is bad, too. Every time we put off something important to do something unimportant, the pressure builds. Things don't get easier; they get harder. As we put tasks off more, we get more stressed and agitated. This affects not only us but also those we love as they feel the pressure based on how we interact with them. Really, nothing good comes from putting things off and wasting time.

So, the natural question is, why do we waste so much time procrastinating?

Immediate vs. delayed gratification

In an experiment conducted on the influence of time on our decisions, researchers offered people a hundred dollars today or a hundred and ten dollars tomorrow. In a second stage, they offered people a hundred dollars in one month from now or a hundred and ten dollars one month and a day from now.

Interestingly, when faced with the immediacy of time, the difference between today and tomorrow, people took the hundred dollars. But when faced with a length of time, they chose the hundred and ten dollars in one month and one day. The findings suggested that when faced with a decision that gives us the ability to plan ahead, we make rational choices, but when faced with a decision that is short-term, we make less rational decisions.

The issue is really one of gratification. If you can get a hundred bucks now, why wait? But if you have to wait a month anyway, what's one more day? The reality is that the decision is still the same: one day's wait. But in the first scenario you can have immediate gratification. The second scenario requires delayed gratification either way.

The principle is the same in every area of our life. As we've talked about a lot in this book, goals are important. And goals are long-term, taking a lot of work to achieve—they are delayed gratification. When things come up in our life that seem more attractive in the present than our goals in the long-term, we often choose immediate gratification.

So, though you may have a long-term goal of being the top salesperson on your team, it's always much more gratifying to check Facebook than to do cold calls. The logical lie we sell ourselves is that we can always make the cold calls later. Of course, we never do.

Different types of procrastinators

In an article entitled, "Procrastination: Ten Things to Know," Hara Estroff Marano writes in *Psychology Today* that there are three types of procrastinators:

Arousal types

These are people who love the rush that comes from waiting until the last minute—think adrenaline junkies.

Avoiders

These are people who are afraid of either failure or success. The fundamental issue is caring too much what others think. "They would rather have others think they lack effort than ability," writes Marano.

Decisional procrastinators

These are people who are deathly afraid of making a decision because they don't want to be the ones responsible for the results.

It's important to study the types of time-wasters and understand the real reason why we behave the way we do. By understanding the motivation behind our procrastination, we can then begin thinking through how we'll change our behavior.

The good news is that anyone can move from time-wasting procrastination to determined productivity. Like anything else, it takes a plan, goals, and determination. It's not easy, but it is essential.

Winners don't waste time

A key component to living a *Fantastic Life* is to understand your long-term goals and to not waste time in your efforts to achieve them. It should go without saying: a fundamental difference between those who are successful and those who are average—or worse—is the ability to overcome procrastination and to manage time in a productive way.

Personally, I think the root of most of our time wasting comes from fear of failure. To me, success is a poor teacher. In real life, we learn mostly from falling on our face. Our attempts to limit failure by doing unimportant things rather than important things are at the core of our decisions to waste time.

Winners understand this. That's why Michael Jordan said, "I've missed more than 9,000 shots in my career. I've lost almost 300 games. Twenty-six times I've been trusted to take the game winning shot and missed. I've failed over and over and over again in my life. And that is why I succeed."

True winners hit the proverbial court each and every day, working hard and constantly to be the best. There are tons of quotes to get us motivated to start going. I like what Walter Hailey has to say: success is defined by "doing what you need to do, when you need to do it. Whether you want to or not." My second mantra is that "success is the process, not the result." I try to find success by doing the process. Getting things done makes me happy.

If you want to win in life and business, if you want to live the *Fantastic Life*, you have to do the same thing.

Stop wasting time and get to work.

Action items

1. Keep a journal for a week on how you spend your time. Track the hours you spend working towards your goals and the hours you spend wasting time doing unimportant things.

2. At the end of the week, analyze the data you've collected.

3. Be honest and decide if you're spending more time procrastinating or being productive.

4. If you're wasting too much time, figure out why.

5. Develop an action plan and habits to be more productive in reaching your goals.

6. Try taking a small Post-It® note and writing your top three daily action items on it. Do those items first thing.

Some helpful questions to ask

1. How am I really spending my time each day?

2. If I'm wasting time, why? What's the real reason?

3. Am I afraid of failure? Why?

4. Am I motivated more by immediate gratification or delayed gratification? Why?

5. What are some things I can do right now to be more productive and waste less time?

Rule #17
Life is About Opportunity, Too

In the early 1990's, Megan Duckett moved from Australia to Los Angeles with one goal in mind: to work in the entertainment industry. To make ends meet, Megan took a job with an event planning company and in her free time she began sewing, making bedding, drapes, and costumes.

With a Halloween event coming up, Megan's employer asked her to make some decorative linings for the inside of some coffins. Megan said yes. It was a turning point in Megan's life when she realized that pursuing her goal of being in the entertainment industry had actually led her to another opportunity: designing props and entertainment decor.

A year later, she got another big break, designing twenty-five silk chandeliers for The Mirage hotel in Las Vegas. By 1996, she was earning more sewing on the side than she was working for the event planning company.

Today, Megan's companies, Sew What? and Rent What?, produce sales in excess of $6 million, and she manages forty-four employees.

She'd never have built such a successful company if she weren't willing to change her plans and goals. Being nimble, as much as planning, allowed Megan to be successful today.

Yes, life is about planning

The majority of this book has focused on the importance of vision, planning, and goal setting. I've focused on these for a reason—that's where most of us fall short. Without a doubt, the *Fantastic Life* is about clearly defining what you want out of life and doing everything you can to plan and achieve your goals. We should always have a vision and a plan for what we want in life and where we're going. We should always be doing everything we can to achieve that plan and those goals.

Life is also about opportunity

But here's the deal: you can't plan everything in life. Sometimes life throws us a curve ball that changes our plans and our goals. We need to be ready for that too.

For instance, when Megan moved from Australia to Los Angeles, it wasn't with the plan to start a multi-million dollar sewing company. No, she wanted to be in the entertainment industry. But as she pursued her dreams, life put another opportunity in front of her that she didn't want to pass up. This happens to us all the time. As we pursue our goals, new opportunities arise.

Earlier in this book, I wrote about how I was privileged to participate in the Tae Kwon Do World Championships as part of the U.S. National Team. I didn't start Tae Kwon Do with the goal to win a world championship. I started with the goal to get a black belt. Funny thing, though, once I had my first black belt, I wanted another one. Once I accomplished that goal, I wanted a third.

In the process of accomplishing the goal of getting my black belts, I showed up, worked hard, stayed focused, and met people who paved the way for my invitation to compete on the U.S. Team. It was only then, when faced with the opportunity to participate in the World Championships, that I formed the goal to win. (I always want to win if I am going to commit.)

At the end of the day, the *Fantastic Life* isn't just about planning; it's also about opportunity and taking advantage of these opportunities as they come our way.

Planning leads to opportunity

Great opportunities, however, don't come our way unless we've already made our plans, set our goals, and begun working towards them. In fact, it's only by taking action on our plans that we discover new and better opportunities that change our plans.

My friend, Jake, is a good example of this. A couple years ago he moved from Phoenix to Seattle to work with a big church as part of the creative team. For over a year, Jake and his wife talked about and planned this move. He thought for sure this was what he'd be doing for a long time. It was a great match for his skills and the next logical step in his career.

But after a few months in the position, Jake met some other creative types, and they began to dream together about forming their own agency. Jake had thought that all the planning he had done in preparation for his move to Seattle was for the opportunity to work at this church, but in reality, it was to open up this completely different and exciting opportunity.

About a year ago he launched his agency with his partners. It was a big risk but today, the agency is successful, having already won awards and some pretty big accounts. But this opportunity would never have come about if Jake hadn't been a disciplined planner and goal setter for many years prior.

As the old saying goes, way leads on to way. When you plan and set goals, working daily to accomplish them, you never know what opportunities will come your way. If you do nothing, though, you'll always know what will come your way—nothing.

One of the interesting things about having clear goals and a focus on what you want is when an opportunity arises you can quickly evaluate if it fits in your future. The road to success is never straight, nor is it flat.

Don't give up and keep moving

So, here's the point. Plan and set goals. Don't give up. Keep moving. But be ready for when unexpected opportunities come, and don't be afraid to change direction when needed. That's the key to the *Fantastic Life*.

Action items

1. Put into practice everything we've talked about in this book about having vision and setting goals.

2. Pursue your vision and goals as if those are the things you'll be doing your whole life.

3. Be ready and receptive to opportunities that may come your way as you pursue your dreams.

4. Loosen your grip on today so that you may see where you can be tomorrow.

5. Don't stop dreaming, but also don't be afraid to have new dreams.

Some helpful questions to ask

1. Am I on autopilot and not seeing opportunities that are in front of me?

2. Are the things I started out pursuing still the things I want to be doing today? If not, why?

3. Are there opportunities in front of me now that I could pursue? If yes, do I want to? What's holding me back?

4. Where in my past has pursuing a goal led to great things I didn't even plan? How'd that make me feel? How can I recapture that feeling?

5. Am I willing to take the risk necessary for bigger reward? Why or why not?

Rule #18
Do Nothing In Moderation

"Moderation is a fatal thing. Nothing succeeds like excess."
— *Oscar Wilde*

Many of the ancient philosophers had a love of moderation. Writing on the concept, the Roman poet, Horace, said:

> You will do better…not to spend your life venturing out too far on the dangerous waters, or, for fear of storms, staying too close to the rocky shoreline. That man does best who chooses the middle way so he doesn't end up living under a roof that's going to ruin, or in some gorgeous mansion everyone envies. The tallest pine shakes

most in a windstorm. The loftiest tower falls down with the loudest crash. The lightning bolt heads straight for the mountaintop.

Translation: don't do anything that gets you noticed because that's when the world will come against you.

Perhaps Horace felt this way because early in his life he made a political misstep, fighting on the losing side with Cesar's assassin, Brutus, in the Battle of Philippi against Antony and Octavian, who later became Augustus. As the battle turned against Brutus, Horace fled, leaving behind his shield. He lost everything, his military career was over, and he returned shamed to court under amnesty from Augustus.

I suppose Horace thought he was doing people a favor by telling them not to put their neck on the line. But was it really good advice? Does it make sense to build our lives around the wisdom of a coward?

Moderation creates mediocrity

For many people, choosing "the middle way," the safe way, is sound advice. I've found that most people are content with flying under the radar. They despise risk. They fear standing for something. They worry about how others perceive them. They're afraid to fail. All they want is the American dream: a house with a white picket fence, a car in the driveway, two kids, weekends off, and a full-cable package.

The problem with living this way is you never get far. Nothing great in life is achieved by being moderate and playing it safe. Columbus would never have discovered the New World if he hadn't ventured into dangerous waters. Lincoln would never have freed the slaves if he'd played it safe. Jordan would never have won championships if he'd stayed in bed when he didn't feel well. All these men understood that they had something important to accomplish, and they knew they'd rather die trying than always wonder, "What if?"

You may not be a famous explorer, politician, or athlete, but if you don't take risks and move away from the middle way, you'll never be one. At the end of the day, moderation in life only leads to a mediocre life.

Do nothing in moderation

In this book, I've shared stories about some amazing people. One thing they all share in common is that none of them have lived a moderate life. Finishing an Olympic race with a torn hamstring is excessive. Playing an NBA championship game with a high fever is excessive. Running the Marathon des Sables is excessive.

As Oscar Wilde said, "Nothing succeeds like excess."

As you've read this book, perhaps you've felt overwhelmed. All these rules are a ton of work. Perhaps fear is in the back of your mind and pulling on your gut. The questions we ask ourselves in this state is, "What if I can't do this, and what if I fail?" Those are the wrong questions. Rather, ask, "How can I do this, and what does it matter if I fail?"

The rules of the *Fantastic Life* might be a total paradigm shift from the way you've been living your life. In the face of such a different way of thinking and doing, it can be easy to dismiss the rules in this book and go on living life as you have all along. That's certainly the safe and easy option.

But I have a question for you, how's your life going? Are you truly happy? Is playing it safe and taking the easy route really working for you? If so, continue on your way. If not, it's time to stop living in moderation and take a full dive into the *Fantastic Life*.

My mantra is, "Do nothing in moderation." In my family, business, athletics, I give my all and more. I'm not content with just average, or even good. These things must be great. Nothing short of this will add up to a *Fantastic Life*. I'd rather try with my all and fail than live a safe life of mediocre "success."

It takes an excessive amount of dedication to know what you want from life, to work on your life résumés continually, to make goals and accomplish them, to be value driven, and to keep moving forward, taking advantage of opportunity as it comes your way. You can't accomplish this in moderation. You have to fully commit and give it your all. You have to be willing to make the sacrifices and to put in the work.

A wise man once told me that when it comes to new ways of living, considering a major change in the way you do things can be like standing on the edge of a great chasm. Until you're on the other side of the chasm and look back, you can't understand what it's like to be on that side. Once you are on the other side, you wonder why you were so afraid to cross the chasm—and how you ever survived living the old way.

Living the lifestyle of no moderation required for the *Fantastic Life* can seem overwhelming at first, but looking from the other side of the chasm, I can tell you it's worth every bit of sacrifice and effort. You can, and should, do it.

It starts today

Perhaps you're thinking, "I'm ready to do this." The temptation will be to start tomorrow. That won't work. That's the path of moderation. Living the *Fantastic Life* begins with the decision to live a life of no moderation, and that starts today.

Today is the day to know your story, be clear on what you want, to cut out what's not important, build your résumés, define your values, and begin planning, making goals, and working towards them. Take a half-day from work if you have to. Schedule out the upcoming weekend to focus on your *Fantastic Life*. No doubt, this will require some hard decisions. You'll be criticized by those who want to play it safe. You'll doubt yourself and be doubted. But don't waste time. Start now.

It's your move

This book is the culmination of everything I've done to be successful. These are lessons learned from the battlefield. It's not easy to live by the rules, but it's essential for true happiness.

The good news is you can do it, and so can anyone else. The truth, however, is most people won't. This is an advantage for you. If you chose to live the rules of the *Fantastic Life*, you can go far simply because you'll be doing so much more than anyone else does.

All it takes is starting.

It's your move. Are you ready to live the *Fantastic Life*?

About the Author

Craig Coppola considers himself a pretty ordinary guy. But to those who know him, he is anything but ordinary. Craig has spent his life setting goals and achieving them— the kind of goals that most of us only dream about. And he's accomplished not one or two, but many of them.

Professionally, Craig was drafted by and played in the Minnesota Twins Baseball organization, won a world championship in Tae Kwon Do, helped build a company to be one of the largest and most successful in his industry, has made a good amount of money, built a strong marriage and side-by-side with his wife, raised four children.

It all sounds too good to be true. Quite fantastic, actually. But the beauty of Craig's life is his solid belief that if he could do it, anyone can. It just takes knowing the secrets to a fantastic life. And that is exactly what readers get through his newest book by the same name, *The Fantastic Life®: How to Get It Live It, And Pass It On®*.

Some may think that it takes money to live a fantastic life, but Craig was not born wealthy. He was not born of privilege. He grew up in a small Arizona town with five brothers and sisters. Throughout his years, Craig built a solid belief that once he decided to do something, doing it half-way was just a waste of time. So no matter what he did, he went for it, a hundred percent, and then some.

That philosophy stuck with him, and it has taken him around the world for business, sport, and adventure. He's scaled mountain peaks literally and figuratively. He's competed in the world's most grueling endurance events, in the world's most challenging climates. He's changed the lives and the fortunes of many of the people he's encountered. And he's built businesses and created jobs by doing as he says, "Nothing in moderation."

The Fantastic Life is Craig's third book. He is also the author of two real estate books, *How to Win In Commercial Real Estate Investing* and *The Art of Commercial Real Estate Leasing*. He speaks to groups about not only his professional experiences and best practices, but also what it takes to succeed and live a fantastic life.

A highly accomplished real estate investor and broker, Craig is the highest producing office broker in Lee & Associates' decades-long history and one of the company's eight founding principals in Arizona. Craig holds the distinguished industry designations of CCIM, SIOR and CRE. He received his MBA from Arizona State University and his BS in Finance from Nicholls State University.